*Tap Once for Yes*

# Tap Once for Yes

## Messages from beyond death

### JACQUIE PARTON

A record of this publication is available from the British Library.

ISBN  978-1-907203-62-6

Typesetting by Wordzworth Ltd
*www.wordzworth.com*

Cover design by Titanium Design Ltd
*www.titaniumdesign.co.uk*

Printed by Lightning Source UK
*www.lightningsource.com*

Cover images by Jacquie Parton and Nigel Peace

Published by Local Legend
*www.local-legend.co.uk*

# Acknowledgements

With deep gratitude to my partner Clive for his unwavering support and love, and to my brothers Tim and Chris, and their families, for being there.

Special thanks to my counsellor Simone Brookes for her sensitive approach to a most unusual case, and to Mary Collinson for her time and effort, inspiring my confidence as a writer from the very beginning.

Thank you Karan Palfreyman, and Jean and Jack Williams, for never judging me. Thank you Penny for listening, and Will and Carly for being Andrew's friends.

This book is dedicated to Andrew,
for giving me the courage to go on by his
constant reassurance that life continues.

# About this book

You will read in these pages a hugely inspiring and joyful account of survival.

This narrative presents extremely strong evidence that the human spirit lives beyond physical death and is able to communicate with and genuinely comfort those who grieve in this life. It is evidence that demands to be taken very seriously.

But not least it is also a story of human courage in facing life's often terrible difficulties, and coming through them all with spirit unbroken and uplifted.

# About the Author

Jacquie spent her early years in Scotland and the West Midlands, before joining the British Army at seventeen. She has had a life full of considerable challenges, from serving in Belfast through several career changes including running her own businesses and retraining as a social worker.

But even more than this, her personal life has been marked by great sadness. Her son Adam died of cot death. She then separated from his father and brought up her first son Andrew alone, proudly seeing him grow into a fine young man who served in the Royal Navy before suddenly and unaccountably committing suicide.

However, Jacquie's story then took a strange and wonderful turn, as from 'the other side' of life Andrew decided to show her that they were still connected...

# Contents

# 1
# *That Day*

'Love knows not depth until the hour of separation.'
—KAHLIL GIBRAN

"Andrew, can you give me a quick call? Ok if you're busy." This was the fourteenth time I had tried to reach him with no response. I was now more than a little anxious because Andrew always either answered or returned my call soonest, however briefly, to allay my concern.

As I tended to my client, I pondered all the occasions in common with many mothers when there had been a delay in contact. The inability to rest or concentrate until the familiar voice of your precious offspring resounded over the `phone, followed closely by the swift abatement of stomach-churning anxiety and frazzled nerve endings settling comfortably back into place.

Andrew lived in a beautifully furnished flat located in one of the more salubrious areas of Buxton. He lived alone, which always amplified my concern because no-one other than him could answer, but to date my fears had been unfounded. This morning was different. Abruptly, I decided against visiting my next client, feeling compelled to set out for Buxton immediately. As I started out on the familiar route from Stoke, driven by something intangible I could not quite fathom, I reflected on the night before.

In the early hours of the morning I had been awoken by a vivid image of Andrew's face seemingly lying flat against something white with his eyes closed. This was then superimposed by the melodic tones of my 'phone jolting me awake. Scrambling to answer it, I was extremely relieved to find that there was no missed call. Thankfully, I wrote it off as a nightmare, as I had thought it to be Andrew calling about some crisis that might have occurred. I went to replace the mobile back on my bedside cabinet, missing the side, delivering it unceremoniously onto the floor.

The next morning, my partner Clive came in to bring me an enlivening cup of coffee (we have snoring issues, so sleep separately). He asked why my mobile was on the floor. I told him of my disturbing nightmare and the relief I'd felt when I realised that there had been no call.

The morning continued as any other: hair, clothes, breakfast, more coffee followed by a brisk walk with the dog around the block and setting off for work at my usual time of 9.30 a.m. ready for my first appointment at 10. I enjoyed my work as a mobile hairdresser, a refreshing change from the dysfunctional world of social work I had left behind some years before. Greeting people with a smile, sharing a chat and a coffee and leaving them with a fresh look and a further booking.

The time that Andrew started work determined the timing of my first daily call. I first called him at 11.50 a.m. At 12.40 p.m. I left him a message, and the time now was 12.55 as I left the outskirts of Stoke. I rang Andrew's father, happily settled with his new wife Sheila of seventeen years in Buxton.

"I can't reach Andrew, have you heard from him?" I asked anxiously.

Sheila, rather surprised at my call, responded that she hadn't but whilst I was driving over she would continue to try and contact him. Clive then 'phoned enquiring after my day following my disturbed night. He sounded a little perplexed as I informed him of my abrupt change of plan for the day; I would speak to him later.

Driving over the somewhat barren moorland hills, its bleakness to me that morning was temporarily made beautified by the warmth of bright sunshine. As I entered the familiar outskirts of Buxton, still not having had a relieving call from Sheila, I tried mentally to articulate why I didn't feel the infant churnings of rising panic. I did not feel I was reacting in the familiar way I felt accustomed to, but neither did I feel normal.

As I drew up to the yawning gateway of Andrew's four storey Victorian building of newly refurbished flats, my eyes fell upon his neatly parked motorbike. Fleetingly relieved at the fact that there had been no accident, my gaze then focussed on his second floor flat as I parked. His spare room light was on, his lounge curtains still drawn. Now, the haunting recollection of last night's possible foreboding premonition played through my mind.

I had no key; I rang all of the six intercoms to gain entrance, with no response. I raced round to an adjoining property, remembering a kind of caretaker, a man Andrew shared his bike interests with - again, no reply. The time was now 1.10 p.m. and Andrew was due to be on duty at the hotel immediately behind where he lived at 2 o'clock. He could just be out, stayed at a friend's house, lost his 'phone; but no, prompted by my dark thoughts I rang 999.

The operator answered in perfunctory fashion. Still a bit perplexed and a little embarrassed at my requesting assistance to locate my twenty-eight year old son, not as yet missing his arrival at work, the word 'police' presented itself.

• • •

A young male police officer, his vehicle parked at the bottom of the awkward driveway, meandered towards me. His face was a little quizzical as to why I'd called the emergency services out as I somewhat awkwardly but nevertheless with conviction expressed my concern that something was very wrong. It was difficult conveying the enormity of my fears as there was no apparent precursor as to why anything would have happened. I did, however, continue to consider that just maybe he had had a brain haemorrhage or stroke, or that maybe his recurrent serious migraine had transposed into something more sinister.

The time taken to decide on breaching the door turned into a good tormenting, teasing forty minutes. I spent most of it tailing the officer as he exchanged radio communications. A female officer joined us, exchanging glances with her colleague, indicating almost indifference to my plight as I implored them to breach the door immediately. It was very apparent to me that my growing distress was quite frankly falling on deaf ears.

It started to rain, a passing cloud compounding the misery of my impotence. The freshly painted green hardwood door was unremittingly impervious to my feeble attempts to slip the lock with my bank card – damn it!

Eventually the control centre had located the caretaker who furnished them with the access code adjacent to the door, releasing master keys. This was it, as with much trepidation I ascended the carpeted stairwell to Andrew's flat between the two officers. The sunshine through the window illuminating our three shadows step by step to the fire door heralded our arrival at my son's flat. Hopefully he would be aware of the commotion that had been caused and remonstrate with me for having caused such nuisance; after all, he had just slept in! On the other hand, the flat could be empty because he had stayed somewhere else.

The three of us stood before Andrew's flat, another delay as the keys failed to open a door barred from within. Exasperated, as my official companions considered retreating to get their 'bunny' (apparently, a term used for a battering ram), I urged the male officer just to kick it in. Without undue hesitation, and probably aware that I would have done it myself now at any cost, the boot of the officer thudded against the unresisting blue wooden door.

The inside bolts, now broken, fell to the floor. The familiar scent of Andrew's favourite plug-in diffuser permeated and accentuated the silence of the flat within. I cast my eyes left, the doorway open to his spare room, the light on, his bike jacket and helmet neatly placed amidst the tidy chaos of temporarily redundant objects and keepsakes. The bathroom adjacent was empty. Slowly, myself still between the two officers, we edged our way up the narrow hallway. His bedroom was next left, his bed turned down as though he'd arisen in the night; 'probably out after all', I thought. The kitchen… straight ahead… door open… nothing was amiss… but then my eyes were pulled directly to the scarf trapped purposefully over the closed lounge door.

"My God, he's hanged himself!"

The dream, his face against something white with his eyes closed, the `phone call in the night announcing his leaving this mortal coil... it was all true!

"He's hanged himself," I stated again bluntly. The male officer stood looking at the back of the door, seemingly stunned and temporarily immobilised. He appeared unsure as to what to do next given that the mother, if right, would face her worst nightmare. I was oblivious to the reaction of the female officer behind as I pushed the door, inviting assistance to overcome the weight of what I guessed to be Andrew's now lifeless form heavily leaning against the other side. The scarf now released, my heart lurched as Andrew's body ricocheted against the door followed by a reverberating thud as he hit the floor.

I appraised the macabre scene from the doorway, unmoving, unnaturally devoid of feeling, a numbness. His now rigor-mortised body, still unblemished. Aside from the scarf tightly wound around his neck, he looked peacefully asleep, clothed in his dressing gown revealing his night garb of white tee-shirt and boxer shorts. God help me. The marble-like stillness of death, the energy of his life now dissipated. I turned and walked slowly back to his breached doorway; standing there, everything looked calm, peaceful and yet nothing could be further from the truth. The two officers, exchanging muted tones, hastily pulling on their blue rubber gloves, standing miles away down the hallway and yet, in actuality, only twenty feet away. I called to them asking if it was too late, though I knew it was more an attempt to make contact as my mind balanced precariously over a mental void.

● ● ●

That morning, my heart died alongside my beloved son.

The policewoman materialised in front of me. "Go and sit in your car," she said. I turned, starting to descend the stairs as I couldn't think of anything better to do; in fact, I couldn't think. Clive called asking me if Andrew was ok, and flatly I told him that Andrew had hung himself. He set out immediately on the forty minute journey from Stoke to Buxton with haste. I considered, in my somewhat stupefied state, that I ought to ring Andrew's place of work and inform them.

"No!" shouted Andrew's colleague as once again I repeated the same distressing line. I rang my brother in Birmingham who started hyperventilating, assuring me he would call back. I rang Andrew's dad and Sheila answered; his dad passed out with shock. I so desperately wanted to reach out and wanted everyone to hear and share my pain. Who else could I ring?

I wandered back up to Andrew's flat, dazedly entering his bedroom to find the female officer going through his cupboards. "Do you know where he kept his clean sheets?" Then, almost embarrassedly, she encouraged me to go back to the car and wait for the ambulance. Directing the ambulance up the pot-holed driveway to the smart little car park, the sun squinting through the tall trees magnified my surreal minute by minute existence. Without introduction, the paramedics ran past me laden down with their equipment, barely acknowledging what they probably perceived as a kindly neighbour giving directions.

I felt like an extra on a film set as a forensic team in white overalls trooped past me, the police line tape fluttering in a now cloudless breeze. Could anybody see me? My name no longer Mum, I felt discarded, side-lined and of no further interest to the automaton service providers.

Clive arrived, drawing close to me, a forlorn little black car in an otherwise empty car park aside from the hastily parked ambulance. He beckoned me in to his car; I slide in expressionless as my head, with somewhat constipated awareness, acknowledged his arrival with Penny the dog. He turned to me, stretching his hand out in tender contact with my leg.

"I'll sort this out, whatever it takes," he assured me.

"Yes dear, I know," I replied, then once more retreated into my heavily barricaded mind.

Penetrating the silence, Clive's voice interrupted, "The medics want a word with you." In my haze, I expected they wanted perhaps to check me over. Wrong! Signatures were required for their paperwork and confirmation of Andrew's doctor. Even within the numbed stupor of my mind, I considered the lack of humanity they extended to a mother's worse nightmare scenario. I felt Clive's apprehension mounting at the magnitude of what he perceived as his unfolding role and task, given the lack of empathy and support extended to us.

Calling at Andrew's dad's flat, no more than a mile from where Andrew lived, I pressed the buzzer of the intercom announcing our arrival. The door opened, my brain now automatically engaging my dulled functioning body, steering me up the tiled stairwell accompanied by Clive to the second floor. Alex, Andrews's dad, his face drawn, pale and defeated, beckoned us inside into the lounge where his wife Sheila sat. Alex had suffered a form of debilitating neuropathy for years badly affecting his ability to walk, but still with as much mustered good grace he offered us coffee. Sheila, herself struggling with a severe chronic breathing condition, struggled to compose herself as we sat down. I had little to say, the morning's event spoke for itself.

Alex chose the denial approach, insisting that Andrew was in fact not dead, but would actually be in touch later as usual. As he clutched his mobile in expectation of the call, Sheila decided on a novel discourse of her four year old nephew's recent activities. Clive sat patiently, proffering polite noises and phrases appropriately. We were all in virgin territory. Time to go; Clive raised himself out of his chair having drained his coffee after we had all now exhausted our disjointed conversations and phrases, politely executed. A family scene devoid of any appropriate narrative - but how were you supposed to act?

The journey back over the moors was in the main silent, as we both struggled with the enormity of the event and the yet to be dealt with aftermath. I could not cry, I dare not start, as this was too big, far too big to handle other than in slivers of a minute at a time. Concentrating on the minutiae that otherwise passed unobserved became my solo occupation. The spider retreating behind the wing mirror of the car, the hairs from the dog that needed picking off my sleeve individually and other such things kept my mind from shutting down as the clock ticked.

Arriving home, Clive grabbed the telephone directories, finding the number of an emergency walk-in centre, keen to stem the approaching storm of anticipated despair. My main preoccupation was to stay in the immediate present, considering neither the minute before nor the minute to follow. Sipping the coffee I had made, I considered its warmth, its sweetness, its comforting familiar taste, its coursing down my throat.

"Let's go," Clive's voice came as an intrusion into the safety of my monosyllabic world.

It was raining. Following the coursing of two independent droplets down the window of the car, I pondered with unnatural depth which would win. Looking out through the metaphorical tears running down the windscreen, I saw glimpses of the past. A woman, toddler in hand, pulling him into a dry shop doorway. A mother with two children creased together as one under the relative safety of a small umbrella whilst a young man strode past purposefully with the vibrancy of youth. My eyes returned to focus on the dog.

I jogged back into real time as the noise of the handbrake announced our arrival at the surgery. Its miserable façade complemented my mood completely. An array of plastic chairs, some taken. "I'll stand outside," I tell Clive. Guided by some imagined agenda of things to do when you find your son hung, here I was. Life was still going on but my perception of it altered in line with my not wanting to participate. But, what option was there?

• • •

My mental health was quite tenuous just now; I could still consider Clive the only reason to continue with life's drama at this moment. I allowed myself to be guided by him from the car park through the drab reception area into an equally austere office. I felt no compulsion to talk as the doctor, weary from a troublesome city surgery, turned to enquire of my problem. Hearing none of the detailed exchanges between Clive and the doctor, I once more marvelled at the contours of the back of the medic's head as he, without pause, tapped out laboriously the events of the day. Satisfying himself of certain key points, dotting i's and crossing t's, a prescription of mind-numbing agents was presented before me. After all, there were people waiting.

Back home again, now early evening. I sit on the sofa which ordinarily felt so comfortable as I normally collapsed into it, kicking my shoes off with well-practised ease, but this time I set myself down as I would a fragile ornament. My normal rituals are abandoned as Clive now guides my schedule, watching and waiting, waiting and watching. With no means of access to my mind, he cannot gauge my contemplations. The `phone rings, I answer, it's the policewoman from this morning. 'Interesting' would be an understatement as I monitored the content of her call.

"Can you arrange to call in at Buxton police station anytime soon and make a statement? Oh, and you could collect some personal effects of Andrew's I've had put in a bag."

Flatly, I inform her that I have no intention of returning to Buxton, let alone the police station. As for his effects, she would have to send them. I sense she is a little put out as she has to consider obtaining her statement. She then decides to drive the twenty miles to Stoke the following evening. How thoughtful!

# 2
# *The Days After*

*'Wisdom is oft-times nearer when we stoop than when we soar.'*

—WILLIAM WORDSWORTH

**Friday 24ᵗʰ June**

Waking from the heavy dreamless sleep induced by exhaustion, I struggle to orientate my senses, the possibility of a waking nightmare swiftly discarded. Clive, my morning cup of coffee in hand, enquires of my night. Normally, a benign ritualistic exchange practised by most people, but on this occasion it feels loaded and I simply reply, "I slept."

My brain is foggy as I enter the bathroom. Looking into the mirror I can barely see my image, instead the mirror becomes a blank canvas for the mirage of mental images that project before me. The explosion of intrusive thoughts of the events of yesterday, the questions, the whys of how it came to this compounded by the deepest of desires to confront him - at least to have been given the chance?

The `phone call two days before had given me no cause for concern. I had rung him directly as he finished work at 3 p.m. - he was just about to go up the road on his bike to get some shopping and would ring me later. At about 7.15 p.m. he called back quite relaxed and looking forward to a quiet evening in; we chatted about the dog I had just collected from the dogs' home and he said he would be up directly at the weekend to see her. I told him I looked forward to his coming and knew he would be impressed with her. I now concentrate on every word he had said, his intonation and inflection, anything at all that belied his state of mind. Too much, too soon.

How on Earth am I going to handle it? In my mind I go back to 1986 to the day I lost Andrew's brother, Adam; he was six months old and passed through cot death. I remember going into the Chapel of Rest at the undertaker's to visit him for the last time. I spent the best part of an hour in there, sitting contemplating outside the door of the room where his little coffin lay draped, inviting me to enter and reveal his still perfect form specially recreated by attendant staff. I spent most of the time in the adjacent toilets looking into the mirror, reaching into whatever depths I could seeking some kind of ill-defined solace. I remember the reflection of my face looking haggard and tired, eyes swollen with tears shed and the thought that came to me that if time were measured in terms of a 12-hour clock, then the time between losing Adam and my joining him was negligible; it would be within the flutter of a butterfly's wing, and we would all be together. With this I felt strong enough to pull back the drape to see my son for the last time, whispering into his tiny ear that I would be with him soon.

I now seek to reproduce some of that feeling as I continue to gaze into the mirror reaffirming to Andrew that I will be with him soon, within the flutter of a butterfly's wing, but not yet. My immediate priority at this moment is somehow to come to a kind of compromise with myself on this insane territory. A decision has to be reached: I either become ill or I get on with it. Sounds simple, but without preparation for this kind of catastrophe, it is!

Each individual has to decide how to negotiate such unknown terrain. They say time is a great healer, and oh how I wish it were five years down the line already. If I go down with it, then five years down the line would have added nothing to my life or anybody else's. Indeed, I would be a far less able person than I am even now, as I still peruse my reflection. Hard as it is, I decide that for now I will remain in the minute. My innate belief that Andrew survived death will keep me strong; I will not question it and I will not doubt it.

The events stand alone, but how you deal with them is something else. Do I let the events control me or do I try and control them?

I thank God for the automatic pilot that resides within me, for I hadn't realised just how capable it was. I allow it to complete my morning ablutions, applying the daily rituals of self-care. Normally I would guide it and participate with interest, but for now I also allow it to manoeuvre me around the house, trusting it completely as it steers me towards the kitchen to make yet another cup of coffee. I glance at the unopened medical prescription, still not remotely interested in its contents or its promise of crisis management in a bottle.

I take over from the autopilot when I see Penny waiting, her little eyes aglow, such a special little dog. A week before when I had selected her, she had been in the first cage. She was howling, a scream that reverberated throughout the kennel complex, a cry from deep within her heart. I had paused, wondering what kind of dog gave rise to such an all-pervading noise. This would not be a dog that was top of my shopping list by any means. As I gazed at this almost awkward looking hybrid black and white dog, its ears creased back as it raised its little head in a piercing cry from the heart, I beckoned to it. The little animal immediately bounded over, her front paws attached themselves awkwardly to the inside of the metal grid, pressing her little chest against the barrier for some desperately sought kind and physical contact. She'd looked older than she perhaps was, and the blackness of her fur had that dusty hue that came from lack of care; she had such a story to tell. This animal was in emotional pain and I felt compelled to get her out. Clive, puzzled, encouraged me to look at the other dogs, but no - my mind was made up, my new companion would be ready within a week. I remember this as I bend down and hug her this morning, for today it is me who silently screams and howls and craves her contact.

Andrew loved dogs, in fact he loved all animals. He used to donate ten pounds a month of his meagre wages to the RSPCA. He had a hamster called Toni, his second after the first one Frank had been tearfully buried with all due hamster honours, wrapped in a sock in the garden. I remember how Andrew became embarrassed if I asked him in public how Toni or Frank was doing, in case anyone overheard; in his small town, people would assume he was gay!

I had often mused about how the autopilot could take me from one location to another destination without me having noticed the journey. I considered this to be a waste of life, and pondered that for our ancestors survival depended on personal focus, as any inattention would have had far more dire consequences than today. I would ask myself who is actually in the driving seat when I have to negotiate each and every minute or the days ahead. Is it the me that steers me through the schedule of the day, or the other me, the 'riding passenger' that interjects with alternatives or objections, interrupting the flow of events unfolding?

Clive busies himself with the practicalities; there are going to be people to see, the flat needs to be emptied and much, much more. There are many things that have to be resolved and there is the funeral to organise. All these issues require my attention and Clive knows it. Like a soon to be shown drama production, he manipulates the setting, the scenes, the schedule, the diary of events and the characters that come and exit the stage. On occasion, he is rather like a well-seasoned P.A. bringing issues to me requiring immediate attention.

They say the eyes are the windows to the soul, but for me they are only the windows to an outside world that now appears so distorted. There is more to do inside my head than there ever was outside of it. Looking down, I have obviously got dressed but did I have breakfast? I can't remember, but I'm sure I must have as Clive would have reminded me had I not, and for now I am heavily reliant on him. An appointment has been booked at the doctor's, another on the list of things-to-do. I decide I will take the dog for a walk before the things-to-do list commences. It is a lovely sunny day and just momentarily the thought comes to me that Andrew would have enjoyed this day out on his motorbike. I put this thought aside as reality calls me back.

There is something strange about this morning, I didn't cry yesterday and I don't feel tearful now. There is certainly no shortage of love for Andrew, he was the most precious thing on this Earth to me and there was nothing that I did not do or would not have done for him. Everything I did for him I did with a passion, as he was my only son. I just feel that he is walking with me, so I decide to follow my instincts and I speak to him.

I say, "What a lovely day it is," and that is where the dialogue starts. I suggest that he might have found it a good day to go for a bike ride and that he could have come up and seen the dog as he had promised the night before on the `phone. As I continue this curious conversation, I notice the dog looking up, as part of the threesome I had formed in my mind. There we are on a family walk, me, Andrew and Penny, in a weird kind of way, but it feels right! It doesn't feel at all unusual and so I decide to enjoy this make-believe world with Andrew. I want just to interact with him normally, not wanting to know why or how the events have come to pass because the future is certainly not up for negotiation. We will stay in the present and enjoy the moment.

Depositing Penny at home, Clive and I make our way to the doctor's surgery just around the corner from where we live. The surgery thankfully is an efficient one, as no sooner am I booked in by the receptionist than my name emblazons itself across the resident television screen, announcing passage to the inner sanctum. I notice first the eyebrows creasing upwardly together in the middle as the doctor turns sympathetically towards us, punctuated by a short intake of breath through her pursed lips as she reads the comprehensive input of notes made the evening before on the computer. It soon becomes apparent, through no fault other than a system that is impotent when presented with anything other than broken bones or severe haemorrhaging, that there is little to be done. Outside exploring the possibility of throwing myself through the surgery window, laughing and foaming at the mouth to highlight the open emotional wound and its toxic contents that have spilled into my life, nothing can be done, although the counselling service will be in touch.

"How long?" Clive enquires.

"Can't really say," the doctor responds, but possibly within two weeks, and of course not to forget the pills.

Again we return home, and at least that one is crossed off the things-to-do list for today. I make us both a drink. I stand in the back garden, visualising Andrew as scenes from the past vividly dance before my eyes. Andrew inspecting newly acquired flowers, and by the garage with his bike, tools in hand as I share a coffee with him.

My mobile sounds as I stand smiling at various recollections. Again, I retreat swiftly behind my autopilot, expecting it to be the police, as I frantically frisk my pockets to take the call. I disengage the autopilot completely as the realisation hits me that my `phone was actually not on me, but still on the windowsill of the lounge. I stand there, a warm feeling accompanied by an eerie intuition. I rush into the house, past Clive lying on the settee, grabbing for my `phone and, inspired, I looked at the call log of the day before. I scan quickly down the numerous attempts of the morning to contact Andrew. Exactly as I had intuitively known, the time I had left him the message "Andrew, can you give me a quick call? Ok if you're busy" was 12.40 p.m. My eyes dart to the mantelpiece, the time now is 12.40 p.m. - absolutely amazing, and one heck of a coincidence! I gush to Clive that I had thought the mobile had rung but that obviously it hadn't, yet the time had uncannily correlated with yesterday's request. I feel sure that Andrew, who had always responded to my calls and rarely let me down, has somehow returned a quick "Ok" call!

I recall this morning when I was taking the dog for a walk, feeling that Andrew was actually with me and looking for an opportunity to confirm to me that indeed he was there. I feel temporarily lifted and my imagination a little exonerated. I stand immobilised by these thoughts, desperately considering possibilities. I feel like I had earlier, rather like entering a room when playing hide and seek with a child - you perceive the presence, but until they are revealed you don't know where. I decide to give in to this sense of presence, because through this I will find a way of going on. I determine that now the choice has to be made, either to 'be ill' or to 'carry on'. With a profound sense of support from Andrew, a new chapter in life will have to begin.

• • •

Clive takes me out around the shops for some fresh air and I have no opinion on the matter, but I do know that the contemplations of this morning seem to have stretched endlessly. What normally would pass as a few hours seems like twelve. I decide to leave Andrew behind; he never used to go shopping with me if he could avoid it, unless of course it was for him.

I have become adept at switching off my emotions, just allowing myself to become an observer. Like a closed circuit television camera swivelling left and right without determination or forethought, just capturing images. I spend a lot of time looking up at the sky, as I just know there is something, but not what it is. This plane of existence doesn't interest me, not now. I really want to know where Andrew now dwells. We enter one of two large bookshops and I make my way to the Spiritual and Philosophical section. I have always been interested in the more esoteric aspects of life, but never with such acute necessity or urgency as I skim over the bookshelves examining one book and then another. With my choice in one hand and my purse in the other, I make my way to the ever-resident bookworm behind the till; this will be the first of many forays to add to what will become quite an extensive book collection.

My brother Tim rings. He doesn't know what to say, but I can tell he has found it a struggle to ring me back.

"When is the funeral?" I don't know at this stage, I have yet to have contact with the undertaker - in fact, I have yet to make contact with a lot of people. There is nothing to say, the stilted exchanges and pregnant pauses hang heavily in the air. I understand. He offers his services in helping to empty Andrew's flat which I gladly accept, though the details in relation to the day and the time I have yet to arrange.

I look up at the clouds again. "For God's sake, if you are there you must help me."

As we return from town, we pass a little Methodist chapel and I search for the name of the pastor or preacher, and then another small church appears, this time Church of England. Again there is the typical board outside the church, and on it a lady vicar listed which I think would be good, so I make a note of her name and number.

Later I will open my door to more sympathetic eyebrows, framing the face of the vicarious angel above a white collar, the badge of religious office.

"Come in, vicar…"

## Saturday 25th June

We always go to Newcastle on a Saturday. It has a nice market town feel, and today would be the first time I would not be looking for additional supplementary items for Andrew. It's difficult to understand why we find ourselves replaying our familiar routine. I expect it is because neither of us have extended family immediately local enough to proffer support, but then grief is a solo activity for the individual. Everyone retreats within the limits of their own comfort zone, with intermittent attempts to interact with sensitivity to the bespoke emotive, arousing and disturbing memories and issues relating to each and every one of us. So, Clive and I find ourselves sharing a coffee in our usual café, when my now irritating mobile alerts me to an incoming call.

Andrew's best friend John has managed to obtain my number, his voice tone incredulous as I temporarily leave the café to take his call. He desperately wants to know if it is actually true, the modulation and inflection of his voice magnifying the sadness of his now changed world. Andrew was to be the best man at his wedding only next month and final preparations had been made, excitement rife with the expectation of this, his most memorable of occasions to date. They had gone for fittings for matching suits, reflecting both the solemnity and of course the splendour of the event, intending to impress with every attention to detail his soon-to-be wife and family. I know that Andrew had looked forward to it eagerly, spoke of it often, voicing various possible amusing anecdotes to sprinkle into his speech, discarding one only in favour of a potentially more embarrassing one for his dear friend. John is still in shock as he offers any assistance he can. I am grateful to accept; the irony for John is that now he will be Andrew's best man.

A whole three-quarters of an hour has passed as I re-join Clive, now more reflective even at this early stage on the many people that will have been left floundering and struggling by Andrew's sudden demise and the circumstances around his death. So many things to think, people to consider, so much pain all round. I defer to my autopilot - just allow one thing at a time, and just do as I say or we will both be in trouble!

Walking into the charity shop, I am lost in thought as I merge with the other shoppers, skilfully presenting a façade of normality. My `phone rings – the police. Apparently, they need to see me about Andrew's life history, a normal practice in these cases. It will only take a few hours. I do not consider three hours as good value for twenty-eight years, and I am thinking quite facetiously, less than impressed with the police this past two days. In fact, I instruct my inner pilot to consider complaining at some more appropriate stage. I make an appointment for next Tuesday, somewhat begrudgingly as I perceive it to be more of an inconvenient interruption. I turn my attention to an old pair of shoes, red with worn heels, and I look at them intensely with animated interest.

We leave the shop and the `phone rings again. The undertaker introduces himself. Andrew is en route to Chesterfield to the coroner's, he will be autopsied there, meanwhile the coroner's officer will be in touch and they will issue an interim death certificate until the full findings are made available. He asks me if I would like him to administer the funeral. I am taken aback as I grapple with the obvious practicalities of death in the coldest of light. I tell him I am unsure, but I think this is borne out of some desire not to face up to this evident necessity. He offers to ring again – I agree…

"What the hell have you done Andrew, what on Earth were you thinking?" I articulate to Clive a passionate mixture of anger, sorrow, love, guilt and ardent desire to have Andrew answer.

Clive responds, "I know, but there were no clues."


## Sunday 26ᵗʰ June

I went to bed yesterday evening offering up my nightly thoughts and prayers, asking for support and solace from whatever source would listen. I requested that if it were possible, could I but hold Andrew in my arms once more, please…

I dreamt this night that Andrew had come to the top of the driveway. He was a boy of thirteen or fourteen years of age, dressed in familiar clothes from that time. I recognised his slight form as he came towards me, a finely striped red and white tee-shirt over his jeans. He looked healthy but dismayed as he closed to me. He put his arms out to me as I reached out to hold him, and I held him tight, reluctant to let him go. My heart was full as I urged him to come with me into the house. "I can't, Mum, I have to go," and with that our grip loosened as he turned and walked away - I knew I couldn't follow, I just knew.

I am a little more buoyant this morning as I recollect my dream. I did feel as though I had held him. I had felt the texture of his tee-shirt and his familiar boyish scent at an age when we would still hug each other before the self-consciousness of adolescence set in, and which I had duly respected.

The literature that the vicar left me has a time frame of grief bracketed into three, six and nine month checklists. A common theme throughout is the propensity to hallucinate with feelings of presence, etcetera. If it happened, I thought, then I would welcome it and enjoy it. I did, however, ponder that even if one does hallucinate, it in no way invalidates the experience or negates its value, nor indeed does it disqualify the reality of the event... does it?

Sundays have always been the day we saw Andrew. Like a ritual we rumbled over the moors with the additional something for him from our Saturday shopping expedition. I always keenly looked forward to it, and depending on whether he was working or not we would often take him for a meal. Speaking every day to him as I did on the `phone, I was up to speed with his recent activities and the ins and outs of his daily work, politics and social agenda. I was always excited to see him. Andrew loved his flat; it was always clean, neat, tidy and well cared for. He basked in comments people passed as they appraised his furnishings and newly acquired gadgets, or indeed his ornaments. He had an eye for beauty and detail which was apparent from the many paintings he laboriously worked on. Inevitably, along with creativity came sensitivity, hence Andrew required more intensive support than would normally be the case for a twenty-eight year old. As a man, he displayed naivety and innocence, struggling in this harsh adult world of ours. This was almost our secret. To his colleagues, friends and acquaintances he presented as extremely balanced, responsible and industrious, and was well-known for his creativity and intelligence. Most of all he was remembered for his kindness and his ability to put others at their ease.

Clive suggests we go for a walk over Barlaston Downs with Penny. The weather is bright and sunny, and its radiance almost feels mocking with its luminosity contrasting our melancholic dispositions. However, with the illuminating soft hues on the mixed foliage and trees you cannot help but stop and wonder at nature's seeming contradictions, so beautiful and yet therein lies its darkness and its promise of shadows. We soldier on, carefully negotiating the aged stile which requires some thoughtful agility, onto the dried mud-laden track flanking a long meandering brook. No-one is about and this pleases us as we start up a small incline. Penny, well-mannered as ever, to which we have grown accustomed, walks dutifully at our side.

Suddenly Penny freezes, her gaze fixed keenly ahead, her ears upright and forward on her upwardly inclined head. We follow her gaze intently, unmoving as she herself has been forced to halt before… what? We are quite uncertain and startled. I am well used to dogs and aware that their sense of hearing is vastly superior to ours. Following her line of sight, the distraction appears to be immediately in front of us, and undeterred by our "Come on" requests, she remains solidly frozen to the spot. We stand, unwilling to break the spell, although with some hesitation I cannot deny the feeling that it is Andrew.

It is like time is suspended as I breathe inwardly "Andrew!" with a rising sense of excitement from deep within my soul at the realisation that he has, as he had promised, come to see the dog. Now, as abruptly as she had halted, Penny continues up the path as though nothing has transpired. Clive and I continue in silence, lost in our own thoughts. The glow created by this encounter persists. I wonder what Clive has made of it but I am reluctant to address it at this time, I don't want to spoil the moment – there are precious few as it is. I proceed to watch Penny keenly should she sense any further presence.

Clive's mobile rings – a family friend. Inwardly I muse to myself as to the nature of this enquiry, probably something along the lines of "Is she dead yet?" "Well, actually, yes," I respond with an imaginary retort! Some of the dead have the misfortune to continue to live, I ruminate, as I meander up the lane to the car to allow Clive some privacy. I never realised how long days could be.

Arriving home, we closet ourselves in the womb-like interior of the lounge. I decide I will surf the Internet for life after death studies and other related esoteric material on forums and websites of interest. Half an hour later, I close the laptop none the wiser or enlightened, and in the main left again to my own general critical skills of human nature and perception. It does however strike me that reading books of a more spiritual nature sparks something deep within me, something very profound that isn't tangible, neither black nor white.

It is almost as though I realise innately that it is the very words we use that get in the way, therefore the truth I am seeking is there already in the shadows; it just has to be accessed in the right way. In many respects at this moment in time, regardless of the content or the esoteric nature of the books I am reading, the true meaning I seek to grasp inevitably conveys itself by hinting at something magnificently subliminal - yet nonetheless real. Their conviction is catching, their feelings contagious. I share my thoughts with Clive from time to time.

"I'm sure you're right," he responds, with hopeful and earnest intonation.

There is nothing remotely distracting on the television, and little of interest to distract me. A composition of brain-rotting reality programmes with a motley crowd of exhibitionists, certainly not a life-enhancing experience; more like fast food for the brain and just as innutritious. Besides which, a variety of world news channels complements our sad dispositions very well. In the absence of good reflective, thought-provoking documentaries, disaster on a worldwide stage is far more befitting. I make us a cup of tea and we retire to bed exhausted.


**Tuesday 28th June**

My memory is not too good lately and this is very much down to the demented world I find myself thrashing about in. As a direct consequence of this, Clive draws my attention to a folder brimming with paperwork, filed methodically with every 'phone call received and every visit and subsequent calling card marked and commented on accordingly. Every bill dealt with and paid for, and Andrew's bank statements also filed. As I leaf through it, he reinforces the importance of recording every interaction with its date and time before I invariably forget about them.

Today I am to see the undertaker to finalise arrangements, and the police, to furnish them with Andrew's history. The vicar is appointed to arrange the order of service and its contents. I take the dog for a walk before the day's activities commence.

"Come in, Neil," as I beckon in the sombre but pleasant-faced young man, his eyes averting downwardly as he passes by me into the lounge. I want to be as succinct as I can, it is difficult enough already. I offer him a cup of coffee as he sits down offering his condolences. Any insurance policy that Andrew had was invalid as he had taken his own life and, although we are dealing with the financial intricacies and complexities of his estate, at the moment this will fall far short of the funeral costs; but this is irrelevant providing it is sensitively and appropriately conducted.

I consider all sorts of formats, exchanging one idea for another. There is a particular piece of music sung in Hebrew called Now We Are Free, one I had earmarked for my own funeral and which I considered emotionally evocative. This is the one thing we will share when I join him from this mortal coil. I also opt for the just as haunting melody of Gabriel's Oboe, and of course the more melancholic processional composition as we enter the crematorium. I do not want flowers. I never really understood flowers at funerals, to be cut down in their prime and left to die with barely a glance of appreciation. However, I will have a rose on his coffin as I had for Adam, his brother.

I am not really interested in the fripperies of the occasion, purely the raw poignancy of a young life extinguished. There will be no additional cars, as I do not need to be marked out in any way as the focal point of this sorry day. The grief is shared. I have lost him over a week ago and the day is for those who have suspended their belief at Andrew's sudden demise, for their own closure and to say their goodbye. I make appropriate notes in my comprehensive folder as Neil respectfully withdraws, leaving me with a date and time, 11.30 on the following Tuesday.

The eyebrows of the plain-clothed police officer introducing himself at the door belie his official capacity. I gesture sweepingly with my arm towards the lounge door. An uncomfortable task for a greying retired policeman extending his working life as a file-builder for tasked officers. His gait and demeanour betray his years, his eyes still animated with keen powers of observation. Sympathetically, he commences with his cup of tea in his hand.

"So, a mother's intuition?" he asks. This question prompts in me an immediate recollection of the haunting vision of the night before, and reflectively I murmur "Yes" - which is largely true.

From here, I try to be as brief as possible, slowly painting a picture of Andrew's character and disposition. Drawing upon my reserves, a collage of his young life soon emerges. I had striven to give him every opportunity, encouraging every project he undertook. At the earliest opportunity, given his age, he had embarked on a series of part-time jobs to supplement his pocket money as he completed his education. Wherever he went he acquitted himself well, always remaining popular with his employers. He had participated in the Air Cadets, the Army Cadets, and also a local contingent of Police Cadets involved with community support projects. He left education with above average qualifications culminating in a BTEC in Travel and Tourism from the local college. With his restless nature, he embarked on a career in the Royal Navy. He was never comfortable being away for long periods of time. He had a girlfriend in Buxton whom he liked to see as frequently as he could, traveling the length and breadth of the country every weekend, money permitting.

He dismissed himself from the Royal Navy, his sole intention being to settle in Buxton as he could enjoy more regular contact with his family. And yes, he did secure work from a local prestigious hotel. With a lovely flat and a comfortable lifestyle, keenly supported and assisted by us, we thought he was well settled. We were completely unaware of the storm clouds that were gathering until perhaps, by a somewhat chemical trick of the brain, the devastating drama was to play out – and the curtains would drop.

Only the week before, he had accompanied us on a visit to Warwick Castle. He would take any opportunity to go out with us. I had bought him a small armoured knight from the gift shop that he had been admiring as a memento. I cannot elaborate any further, neither do I wish to. No more to add, it is enough just living with it day to day, without having it recorded on police files.

I have not been at all enamoured with the police since the event thus far; however, I do make an exception for this kindly man. Never once deviating from the job in hand, he proceeds both diligently and yet compassionately. It is strange that extending compassion is re-marked upon instead of being taken as a given. These interviews, he acknowledges, can be difficult. I thank him for his kindness along with his departing condolences – the mandatory exercise now gently and respectfully concluded.

With one more meeting outstanding, I turn my attention to Penny and her obvious desire, given her reposed posture; I administer a full body massage.

With my empty coffee cup in hand I answer the door to the vicar, returning to the kitchen for a refill plus two. This will not be a cucumber sandwich moment, as I re-join Clive on the sofa. I am so exhausted with it all now, I cannot really think. Having furnished the vicar with the three pieces of music I have determined suitable, I field the remainder of the service back to the patient and receptive cleric to deal with. At this moment, Clive interjects, reining in my unreasonable address. The gentle man, sensitive to my weariness, offers to return at another time. Clive continues, reminding me that this is to be the final testament to Andrew. Both I and my now dimly flickering autopilot sit slumped together on the settee. I sit in a trance, trusting Clive implicitly to finalise the arrangements of the funeral, allowing the swell of conversing exchanges to wash over me like the ebb and flow of the tide as it washes over jagged rocks. Arousing me from a metaphoric screensaver, the vicar departs.

The date to be carved into my soul forever will be Tuesday the 5th of July, 2011 … and so let it be.

# 3
# *The Funeral*

'*Do not stand at my grave and weep; I am not there. I do not sleep...*'
—MARY FRYE

The sun betrays its presence through a gap in the curtain, lighting up the otherwise dark sanctity of my bedroom. Three little stuffed toys, one bear dressed in traditional Portuguese attire, another with its blue nose sniffing into a towel, the third an old-fashioned antiquated rag doll, look down at me from the top shelf; presents for bygone birthdays from Andrew. Their glassy-eyed stares mesmerise me as I implore Andrew, "Please be with me today." I beseech him from the bottom of my heart to walk with me subliminally – just to be there. I don't feel lonely; I haven't felt lonely, it's only that today feels almost like a ritualistic interruption between Andrew and our relationship. The sooner this is over, the sooner I shall be freer to explore my new-found affinity and subtle bond with my son.

I take out my newly acquired purchases of suitable clothing for the funeral, the carefully chosen dark blouse with a tasteful overlaying of small, almost like Forget-Me-Not flowers, accompanied by dark trousers. They are a nice combination, pleasing at any other time, but today their purpose alone is to look smart. I have always tried to look smart for Andrew, always wanting him to be proud of any impromptu introduction to one of his many friends or colleagues at work. I still want him to be proud of his mother as today this will be my last appearance to the world as Andrew's mum. The three stuffed toys look on with conspiratorial approval.

Yesterday I saw Andrew for the last time. I had requested that he be dressed and placed in the Chapel of Rest at the undertaker's for anybody who felt they needed to see him for their own closure. I had had to decide if I wanted to see him, and decided I would. I was the first to see him into the world and I felt compelled to ensure I would be the last to see him leave it, though my heart was heavy.

Once more, the journey to Buxton, a strange affair invoking memories of the last time I had made this excursion unknowing its final destination and branding of my soul. Clive, forever protective, tried to dissuade me from seeing him – but this had to be my call because it would be an image I would take with me. A surreal journey in an otherwise bizarre day. The car stopped, the engine now silent, the handbrake in place. The undertaker's yawning driveway, a silver grey hearse parked in an open garage as we slowly walked up the gravelled pathway towards the otherwise unremarkable building. Just the door between me and my son, I had to do this, I had to do this.

The girl behind the desk looked up at me, having expected my arrival, her face projecting a picture of compassion as her eyes locked with mine. I noticed the customary eyebrows once more merging upwardly across the bridge of her nose. She arose from her chair beckoning me to follow her through the nearby door to her left; few words were now exchanged as I mutely walked behind her leaving Clive sitting in the small waiting area. Immediately through the door, another directly ahead, I paused in the passage turning to the right, staring down the length of the small corridor. I noticed a window at the bottom, the sunlight streaming through, bouncing off each of the four brass door handles to who knows what despair lying behind them.

I barely acknowledged the door now opening directly to the left of me. Remaining half-turned, I now moved my gaze left. I saw Andrew from the doorway, the greyish pallor amplified by the darkened, curtained interior of the Spartan room. My body betrayed my hesitancy, but by the same token there was a necessity to see and touch him for the last time. I edged round the side of the coffin, taking in every detail – the coffin itself, its handles and the capsule that contained my son. He was wearing a dark blue suit I had bought him for interviews when he left the Navy, a white shirt and a dark blue tie. I remember him posing in the shop mirror as he modelled himself back and front determining the fit and its suitability for a forthcoming family wedding. Andrew always liked to look well turned out; I now smiled with irony as I considered how he still looked smart. If it were not for the blueness of his fingers and his ears and the still gauntness of death, I could have mistaken him for being asleep. I noticed the top of his head was draped with some of the interior dressing of the coffin; the by-product of a post mortem had necessitated this stroke of creativity. My whole life had been about keeping my boy safe and well; how precarious our life and existence.

I traced every inch of his face with my fingers, in fond remembrance of times I had done this when he was alive and in fond memory of his growing from a boy to a man. His bright blue eyes were concealed from me now; I took his hands, first his left and then his right. I noticed his neatly manicured fingernails sunken within the blue of his fingertips – I kissed his fingers as I looked into his face. "You stupid boy." I ran my hand the length of his leg up to his chest, pausing before where his heart would have beaten, his body now rigid, no warmth, no give. The tears ran from my face dropping from my face to his. As I bent down, I kissed his forehead still clasping his hand. "Goodnight sweetheart, sleep well."

I was fairly composed until I got outside and once again saw the hearse parked – I started to cry. Through my blurred eyes I could see opposite the antiquated chapel; it was there before I was born and it will be there long after I too am gone. It had been privy to so many lives lived, the confidante of many traumas. People are indeed fortunate if they are certain of the church's doctrines and dogmas; I consider them a short-cut to the universal truth, as to my mind all leads to the same source. All my life I could never make anything just fit for convenience or any reason, it had to resonate with me instinctively and intuitively. If the divine spark dwelt within that building, then let me feel it now! If it had any compassion, it would see me now. I am sure this same cry echoes through eternity. Travelling back through the city of Stoke, the spires of churches could be seen to reach up towards the sky. I look beyond; the promise for me lay above the spires, not below or within these vestiges of respite.

Opening the door on arrival at home, we were greeted by the newly-appointed nurse Penny. Her head rose in anticipation with a well-rehearsed and practised dog-style smile, showing all her teeth causing Clive and I both to break with our philosophical thoughts and reflections. Little Penny, a bridge between two lame ducks. Clive and I laughed, momentarily distracted by her ministrations. The day before Andrew's passing I had collected her en route from work, and at about half-three in the afternoon I had brought her home. She was keen to remain with us all the time, always trying to understand – her eyes directly engaging with ours. When Clive had arrived home, she greeted him in the kitchen; it was like we'd had her for years, really strange. Penny was what was called a Kojack, crossed between a corgi and a Jack Russell with longer legs, her ears upright and ever alert, readily folding down like umbrellas in anticipation of attention. Clive had said to her in the kitchen as she sat before him gazing intently up, "What have you come for? You've come for a reason." Those words echo to this day as we looked at her now still contorted human-like smile.

She showed no favouritism between Clive and me, attending to us in equal measures as though engaging with two puppies she had acquired. She was a very special little dog. Barney came to mind as our spirits were temporarily lifted - my little Jack Russell, a dog with extremely challenging behaviour from the day he was born. The dog, had he been human, would have been locked up as a delinquent lager lout years ago; he had no finesse, no grace. I blame myself, it must have been a bad upbringing, indulged but not trained, but I loved him and all the nineteen years we spent together. If he had had the ability, he would have had Clive's clothes stuffed in bin bags and on the lawn, never quite understanding where he really figured in the scheme of things. My little dog had been put down the week before Penny had arrived.

Such was the gap in my life that Clive had insisted that we went to the local dogs' home. I was fairly reluctant at first, as my affection for Barney had been great and I didn't think for one moment that he could be replaced by a whimsical purchase. So I was completely taken aback when I returned with a receipt in hand for Penny, to be discharged a week later complete with full medical and injections. Penny on the other hand had enough love for all humankind, gently arising as people came to the door and greeting them. Then at some time during the interactive exchanges she would appear somehow – underneath a hand, on top of a lap, absorbing every bit of pleasure as it presented itself. Suddenly you found yourself looking into not one set of eyes but two, as Penny had ensconced herself, participating in this new trialogue she had formed. We could not help but love this beautiful animal – a gift at any time!

• • •

I take the dog for a stroll around the block, deciding that the resident pilot can conduct me through most of the day. I will emerge relatively safely from this remarkable faculty I have come to rely on as and when I need to. Family are starting to arrive; two brothers, one from Birmingham, the other from Manchester, and their families. The house slowly fills up and I retreat to the back garden. Although cards have been gratefully received, these extensions of heartfelt commiserations sit in a pile and I have barely glanced at them.

It occurs to me that it is not so much about resting in peace – it's about those who remain behind who attempt to live at peace. I am sure that Andrew, arriving on the other side, would have regretted his action immediately; but unfortunately it is a one-way ticket.

I consider that two of the most stupid phrases I have ever heard are the following. The first one is, "It was very brave thing to do" - because how could you hang yourself? I immediately feel compelled to remind them that they can in no way identify with the mental torment of a suicide; rational decision is unlikely to have to have come into the equation. Bravery is based on an altruistic decision. The other phrase, although often dressed up in alternative language, is "It was a cowardly thing to do." Once more the same response is demanded, although I do add that cowardice is more appropriate to self-preservation and not your own annihilation.

Some people are drawn in voyeuristic fashion to know the ins and outs and its emotional impact, their excitement almost palpable from the avid interest they display in their presently smug inviolate world – I am sensitive to this, terminating any further discussion.

I stand and look through the garage window, shielded metaphorically by the veil of glass, once more appraising my son's belongings. "I loved you so much, sweetheart." Having myself been adopted, Andrew had been my only living genetic link. I had stored up fantasies of a new ancestral tree. My contemplative preparations for the forthcoming emotional battle are interrupted by the sound of the vicar's voice as he closes behind me. I continue to gaze through the window as I address his empathetic presence.

"Why do I feel so calm and peaceful?"

He reflects back, "It is early."

With this, I turn and proceed towards the house to greet the accumulating throng of unhappy guests and family. Never had a houseful of people been so quiet.

They allow me the space to move around without interruption, passing the odd comment and infrequent exchange. Not out of any sense of politeness on my part, for anything I do is completely motivated by any instinctive skills I can utilise to get me through the day. Clive is very adept at the polite formalities, bustling to and fro with mugs of coffee ably assisted by everybody present.

The now heightened voices alert me to the arrival of the metallic silver grey hearse. Glancing out of the window I glimpse the Royal Naval ensign flag draped over the coffin, with its condemned English red rose laid carefully upon it. I feel the muscles of my heart constricting, struggling to stop it breaking asunder. With all the strength I can muster, I strain to stifle my natural tendency to break down with all-consuming grief. Today is to be conducted with dignity and decorum; it is not for any indulgence on my part to distract from the proceedings of this morning. All our thoughts this morning must be centred on him, to ensure his peaceful departure and arrival at who knows where; for the moment it will suffice if he will walk with me.

Neil the undertaker, now at the door with his officious ribboned top hat underneath his arm, informs me we are ready. I turn to Andrew's best friend John to announce our departure. John has shouldered something of a supportive role for us, conveying date and time to many of Andrew's friends and colleagues and referring numbers to cater for back to me. The numbers climbed in excess of our original order, amounting to a three fish and two loaves scenario. I had now additionally, tongue in cheek, put him in charge of rations.

Without hesitation I now grab my handbag and march towards the car, patiently waiting as Clive secures the house and now joins me. Neil, in an obviously well-practised and almost archaic manner, his top hat still ceremoniously in hand, paces slowly the mandatory twenty or so feet ahead of the hearse, announcing to the world the darkness within this house, Andrew's home. Off we go, nose to bumper like some inorganic snake winding its way down the hill and around the periphery of the town some two miles or so.

The surreal act is about to commence. The hearse passes the gated opening to the crematorium, and Clive and I now take the lead. Parking next to the venue, a short walk finds us outside the tall crematorium doors. Approximately fifteen devastated individuals await the arrival of Andrew, the first time he has ever been late. I am nonplussed by the delay, it is not the time for pedantic protocol. It is the kindly intended ministrations that count.

Coffin bearers in place, the doors are open and the vicar takes his first step as the opening chord of the most beautifully arranged music echoes from within. Its harmonious rises and falls denote deep reverence through stifled sobs and jagged cries from those behind me and those seated as we pass. I feel extremely overwhelmed and touched by the number of people who have been awaiting our arrival, as I concentrate on resolutely placing first my right foot followed by my left and so on. No-one that knew him attempts to embrace me or put a supportive arm about my shoulders, though contact will be freely available should my resolve crumble. As ever, I am conscious of being watched which only serves to reinforce me, strengthening my reserves. I draw strength from their belief in my fortitude – let the service commence.

In my mind, I leave the crematorium, I let my spirit wander. I think of scenes where Andrew did not feature. I think of holidays that Clive and I have shared, I think about my days in the army, where you aren't paid to think. I patrol the streets of Northern Ireland once more, horse-riding on a sunny day, laughing with a friend as we dip our legs into a crystal clear stream, marvelling at the panoramic beauty of the countryside and sharing our youthful exuberance to rejoice in the moment. Back dropped though it is by the sound of blown noses and soft crying.

I find myself going further within as the vicar speaks of Andrew's life. I hear of his earlier ambitions to become a magician, well-practised as he had become with sleight of hand, but this was for other people to learn who hadn't known him as he grew. I'm walking on a sandy beach, looking out to sea, when the haunting rendition of Gabriel's Oboe permeates my senses. This is a soundtrack that has been lifted from a film called The Mission, played in a certain part when missionaries were embarking up dense jungle waterways into the mist. In my mind's eye, I see Andrew casting off, his face becoming more obscure as he departs further into the etheric fog.

Now, the beatitudes... blessed are the poor... the meek... the humble? I don't think so. If this were the case, why is the world run by a bunch of psychopaths? In any event, if those are the attributes we must aspire to, to know God, then why, I question, should you get to know God before those who plunder our souls?

Now, the finale. Although the song is not sung in English, I know its lyric off by heart. To me, its magnificent composition is made more beautiful by its Hebrew accentuation. The translation is there for those who wish to follow its lilting synchronisation, but for me:

*"We regret our sins, but...*
*we sow our own fate*
*and under my face I remain feeble,*
*under my face, I smile."*

Its promise of unity with an all-unifying source reverberated within my being:

*"Almighty freedom,*
*almighty freer of the soul,*
*be free, be free*
*and imagine...*
*Free with peace at last,*
*it's lovely,*
*it's lovely, this land..."*

I merge completely with Andrew's spirit as the words resound around the chapel, my eyes rising from the coffin to the illuminated stained glass windows, the rays of sun penetrating the darkened recesses. The strings and underlying heartbeats of the soft drums tease the spirit, drawing it upwards to seek the light, making one almost expectant of some kind of epiphany. My chosen masterpiece is drawing to a close:

*"I should have been there*
*with them*
*when the world crashed down,*
*but now*
*they must rest in peace with me."*

Do they feel it as I do? I had opted for no hymns as I did not want people distracted by words they did not recognise, let alone have to sing. No, I want their spirits to absorb pure, raw emotion. I need them to reflect in that short time on the illusion that is life. I want their minds to meld as one and focus through evocative harmonies on the true essence and nature of the realms beyond. Without disruption or diversion, they will emerge more contemplative.

Now the committal. "Don't go, not yet." A pregnant pause follows, a problem has occurred; prompted by the eyes of the vicar, Neil the undertaker walks directly across to us. For some reason, the coffin will not lower. Both Clive and I nod in affirmation that the people be led quietly from the chapel. I move towards the still draped coffin. I pick up the red rose discreetly; I raise it to my lips, kissing its soft petals reliving in its deputising way a profound desire to caress my son one final time. As I replace the merciful bloom, the mechanism of the coffined platform whirrs gently into action. Lost as I am in the moment, I still find the words "That's odd" cross my mind briefly.

The chapel is empty as I return to the glare of the day. The people gather about me. I recognise few, although they themselves have obviously seen me often with Andrew. I embrace them back thankfully, sharing with Andrew's shadow my heartfelt appreciation of the enormous show of support they display. The whole of the hotel staff have attended, which I truly had not expected. Many of his colleagues are still genuinely and demonstrably shocked as they solemnly but sincerely voice their condolences. It is very apparent that everyone here has been affected in some way quite gravely, reflecting some incident, conversation or last exchange they had enjoyed or shared with Andrew; not one can cast any light on the catastrophe leading up to this day.

Everyone is invited to the small venue where a buffet and adjacent bar we have booked for the occasion await our arrival. A beautiful leather-bound book of remembrance is presented to me. As I turn the pages, there are not just names and commiserations, but full letters of testament and endearment to someone who had touched lives in so many ways. Why did he keep his contemplative misery to himself, or indeed how?

My family beckon me to join them; I decline. I'm managing quite well, thank you, behind my reinforced ramparts and imagined impenetrable walls. I stand immediately beside the coffee jug as I deal with an upwelling of obscure feelings. I seek not to try and understand why I find myself drawn to reading the notice board. I really need to make an effort. Glancing around the room, I notice a long banqueting table. The hotel manager stands adjacent, observing, overlooking, with almost symbolically his entire staff seated at the table. Unfalteringly, I draw towards them, I need to speak to them one last time. All conversation now stilled, they raise their eyes towards me expectantly. With heartfelt feeling, I tell them how extremely touched I am and that it is good to see their familiar faces. I struggle to quell the party's efforts and desire to proffer appropriate sentiments, attempting to defuse the difficulty with of course forced humour. I turn dramatically to the hotel manager, replicating Andrew's dry humour for which he had been renowned, and say, "Andrew would say 'I told you I should have been given that promotion'." This dissipates the heaviness briefly, provoking laughter as I turn and walk away.

I now turn my attention to Andrew's best friend, John, and his once line manager, Will, exchanging mutual anecdotes. Between them sits a drink, a Bacardi and Coke; this would be the last drink ever bought for Andrew. I leave them with an open invitation to come back to the house with us for a final cup of coffee.

Clive and I return home, expecting my two brothers and their families for the final rendezvous. John and his fiancée also join us. I feel myself physically wilting as my adrenalin subsides. The funeral went well, it is agreed.

With some hesitation, John suddenly asks if Andrew has left any letters. I say "No", enquiring why he asks. He seems unsure about continuing so I encourage him to finish. He speaks of a dream he has had which was extremely vivid. The room falls silent as he expands on the detail. In the dream, he and his fiancée had entered their house to find a letter had been delivered. He had picked it up, opened it and read it – a letter in Andrew's handwriting:

*Dear John,*

*By the time you receive this, I shall be gone.*
*I am so sorry about the wedding.*
*Please find enclosed a cheque for the suit.**

*Andrew*

(* referring to a suit measured for his role as best man)

At this, John had dropped the letter in complete shock, prompting him to awake immediately and sit up, sweating profusely and sharing this experience with his fiancée, now roused from her own sleep. It had appeared very real to John and had shaken him considerably; in fact, it still haunted him.

I immediately accept that Andrew had reached out to John, trying to affirm to his friend some form of intelligent survival in a way that was personal to his friend. John himself had never considered spirituality, still thoroughly engaged with life as young people are. Caught up in life's distractions, he had not felt the need as yet. However, his fiancée and I are of like mind.

As he relays his story, we all sit reverently nodding as we appraise this possible evidence of survival. When he finishes, we silently allow it to be the closing thought and frame for the day as we say our goodbyes.

# 4
## *Tap Once For Yes*

*'I do not believe... I know.'*

—CARL GUSTAV JUNG

I continually satisfied my growing hunger with books of contact and interaction beyond the grave. I explored different religions, variations, combinations, the philosophies and histories. With fervent passion I sought to discover for myself the origin of belief and humankind's quest to ascertain and realise the universal truth. At the end of the day though, for all the books on spirituality that I examined - at least, all the generic ones off the shelf I had read in the various bookshops I had frequented – I was left with a problem. The difficulty was that I only had other people's opinions or experiences to go on – a dilemma for me! If there was a way for me to find a truth, then I had to find it myself - but how? Well, that remained to be seen. If it took until the day I died, I would satisfy myself that I would be joining him.

There it is, the temple of knowledge, the better of two big bookshops in town. At least, the only reservoir of learning I had access to at this moment. I would sooner have had admission to the Akashic Record, the field of all that has been and all that is and ever shall be. But for now I relied on my intuition to guide me as I thumbed through the shelves. Clive, well used to these forays, looked on as I embarked on choosing my next big reading project. It would be one of the bigger and heavier books, and certainly one of the more thought-provoking ones; then his customary tut tut at the price as I made my way to the till. I would feel the rush of possibilities that my new book might offer. I would say to him as I passed, "If the book appeals, I do the deal." Clive could not argue with that, it would probably be more akin to dragging a starving dog away from its meal.

My eyes on one occasion were drawn to the bottom shelf, tarot cards, angel cards and goodness-knows-what cards. Various promises in a box. But then I saw the pendulum. I had heard about pendulums in terms of their abilities to divine potential properties. This was a pendulum that came on a chain, complete with a starter's guide, Pendulum For Beginners; my eyes lit up at this possibility, one that I had yet not explored – I thought I would try it. Deal done.

Clive was probably very aware of my deep soul searching yearnings to make contact with Andrew, although he never discussed it or mentioned it; he was as ever in the background just watching. If I could gain solace from anything then Clive was a keen supporter; if it alleviated in any way the chronic pain of emotional loss, he would have bought it in abundance.

I would have been quite happy to return directly home, but for now we somehow had the façade of normality to maintain. We went round the big shops, my hand nervously grasping the contents of my plastic carrier bag, momentarily inspired with anticipation of possible contact with Andrew. I would talk to him as soon as we got home, in the back garden; I would tell him of my intention to contact him that evening, when all was quiet. Our house was detached, so all would be quiet. I had figured that if I gave him notice of my intention, somehow he would arrange to be there in whichever way he could and attempt to talk with me. This feeling was quite deep seated and profound, knowing somehow that I was on the precipice of communication, knowing I just had to find the right mode. Maybe this was it!

• • •

I seem to spend most of my time flitting in and out of the present, addressing images, thoughts, philosophies. Strange, as I look round, maybe in another time and another place, I wonder if I would have noticed the odd kind of me. Probably not. I had been fully engaged most of my life, but as you get older there comes a time when most people give pause for thought. When crisis hits, it is then you find out where your strengths lie and what you really believe, or don't, as the case may be. How many people was I passing that are experiencing some calamity or disaster in their life? Can you tell from their faces? Not always. Can you tell from their demeanour? Perhaps. Individuals can be trampled by a whole herd of sheeple going about their daily activities, their work, taking their kids to school, meeting that appointment, hitting that target. I wonder if they ever stop to think.

I muse about this trendy word 'target'; every target met is really a person, for without people there are no targets. Quantity of targets has replaced quality of service, and is reflected in our culture. These concepts have never become more apparent to me than now when brought to bear by priorities magnified - infinitely magnified. My eyes look on, but my spirit does the wandering; I close in on people, I try to feel what it is they have lost in their materialistic frenzies of the moment. A lot of people appear to go about their everyday activities like battery chickens. If you go into a supermarket or a cheap clothing chain store it is never more apparent; their eyes are glazed, scanning back and forth for the cheapest sources of the ever-depleting resources of our world.

Going back a hundred years ago, anybody who could write, produce, craft, paint or create would be defined by that talent and their own satisfaction. An endless sense of wonderment for the purchaser or receiver proudly displaying their newly acquired possession; but, thanks to mass production, the human need to be accomplished or indulge any flair, imagination, inventiveness they may have been born with has been denigrated, thwarting any expansion or development of self in terms of knowledge and self-realisation. One could be someone in those days, known for something in one's own right, not in terms of monetary resources, and certainly for us the common people not a life founded on virtual capital. To be appreciated and to have regard for others, that in itself is priceless. It appears to me that in today's society it is more about what you look like and have than what you are and who you are - your talents, your qualities, your morality and character. There was a time when your opinion would have counted, but today it seems that individualism is no longer appreciated. A blanket policy is applied to all and sundry regardless of the particular individual, more akin to entity management in the name of anti-discriminatory policy.

People have had their entitlement to be an individual eradicated by legislation and political correctness, which in itself is a bit of a contradiction because you can hardly be both political and correct in the same sentence, as politics by its nature is bias and generally in the interest of the few. There are no answers, no easy answers; unfortunately, the world is not driven by the really thoughtful, considered, considerate majority of intelligent fore-thinkers. The world's influence is held by a minority of economic interests, driven by desire for power and control and devoid of spiritual input. They only feign allegiance to some universal God when it suits them and serves their purpose. Truly spiritual people do not pursue or crave power.

I remember when I was young overhearing that "People are like mushrooms, spread with muck and kept in the dark"; how can people be different when they have to negotiate the sludge of bureaucracy? How can they find themselves or help each other if they too are floundering in a fog of uncertainty in an unstable world? My political ruminations and deliberations ran their course deftly through my mind as I simulated normal shopping practice of window-gazing and animated interest in my surroundings. Soon, I shall be home…

Home at last. I made a coffee as I considered what I needed to do before doing what I wanted to do. Still, I was dealing with the debris left behind by Andrew: British Telecom, the electricity and gas companies to name but a few. The ineptitude of call centres never fails to amaze me, but neither do they surprise me. It took an average of two or three attempts to resolve issues relating to Andrew's outstanding debts. Always I was assured by some Tracy, Dave or Tony that they would themselves deal with it specifically and put an end to the round of continuous questions. Invariably I always seemed to get the amnesiacs or at least the young people in the very early stages of Alzheimer's. Of course, it barely affected me as generally the autopilot was dealing with it as I had other things to think about, except for the odd occasion it had to seek clarification with me.

On one particular occasion, I hastily pushed my pilot aside to address one young man on the `phone who addressed me as Mr Parton and asked why I could not pay my bill. He was fortunate of course that we were separated by a vast expanse of land and sea between us; had he been across a desk, I think I would perhaps have been arrested. Compounding it of course was that David actually worked in India, and his appointed accessible name was not remotely compatible with his ability to communicate or speak English. Whereas in the more recent past I would have displayed more patience, on this occasion I think I lost it. My rabid assault on his organisation and their inability to handle the most simple of requests was lost on this daytime target shuffler. To give the unfortunate man his due, having grasped the scenario he did sympathetically conclude the outstanding business of thirty-nine pounds and three pence. Another coffee ...

The garage had become a no-go area for me. A small assembly of Andrew's affects stood at the end. The assorted collection of his paint brushes and paints, his easel, photographs, mail and some CDs sat eclectically among the hastily packed bags of clothes and bedding, untouched since the day that Clive and my brother had made the miserable journey to retrieve them. I had insisted that my brother take any domestic equipment and effects and use them, or maybe distribute them around his family. I had no further interest other than this somewhat material heap of memories, the emotionally evocative personal belongings that belonged to my son. When I look through the window of the garage, I spy his large black suitcase which I had purchased with care, considering its durability for his new career in the Royal Navy – how proud he had been on completion of his basic training. The kettle he had purchased in haste to replace his old leaking one standing idly upon his rolled kitchen mat. I stand as if shielded from the emotional overload by the wall between us staring at these, the redundant items of his and indeed our life together and apart.

Sometimes, I did make brief forays into the garage, bravely. I rummaged through his plastic storage drawers to find something poignant almost as a tease to my emotional reserves - to touch something, to caress it only to put it back. If it became too intense for me I would beat a hasty retreat, sometimes with another token in hand to hide in the house, bringing them home piecemeal like my fragmented emotions. I would feel like a cracked vase trying to repair itself.

• • •

I turned my attention to my little box with the pendulum inside. I took out its contents, a little brass pendulum on a chain, a little book outlining a guide to basic dowsing. I invited Clive to participate and with patience he sat with rapt attention. The object of the lesson was to divine the flip of a coin. With tenacity I repeated the experiment to try and determine the outcome of the coin as it fell. My quest to become a master diviner within half an hour was not promising, so I moved on to lesson two. The object of this lesson was to locate an object that Clive would conceal in the lounge and I would divine where it lay or was hidden. I wasn't being particularly successful, but fully engaged as I was with my agenda of this moment I implored Andrew to help me, just to guide me. "How do we communicate?"

I went to make a drink, deciding to spend the remainder of the afternoon ensconced on the couch with one of my recent reading acquisitions, choosing to read one of my more spiritual books and pander to my present inclinations. I perused the chapters on the spirit's ability to remain around and pondered their necessity to make contact, reflecting on my earlier feelings. The scenes unfolded, looming in my memory with extraordinary resolution. I thought in the first instance about the vivid premonition and the compulsion that had instigated my arriving in Buxton. I considered the strong feeling of presence and the hallucinatory ring on my mobile correlating exactly to the time of the message I had left. The seemingly sentient visitation by Andrew as Clive and I had walked the dog. Those first two weeks, culminating in the coffin refusing to lower, only for it to start to descend when I had replaced the rose. There appeared to be a pattern forming. I recognised that disbelief prevents people from seeing what they don't want to, but conversely belief can facilitate people seeing what they do want to. Yet this in no way negates the reality when I consider how little our senses pick up on until we are thoroughly engaged with a project. For instance, how many red Volkswagens had you noticed on the road until you had one?

I had enjoyed the dreams. The extremely convincing dreams other people had experienced and shared with me. Maybe the light we seek burns relentlessly at the edge of the shadows.

The `phone rang. I was informed by the police that Andrew passed between midnight and 0200 hours on the morning of the 23$^{rd}$ of June. This would be approximately the time of my precognition. Andrew, through some form of quantum entanglement, had alerted me to his intractable fate. With this revelation, I remembered Sheila telling me at the funeral that the electric clock in their flat had stopped at about 12.30. Stranger still was that the watch I had passed to Andrew's father was stopped at 12.30 when he had taken it out of his pocket at home.

There was something just teasingly beyond my grasp. I don't doubt it appeared to be an impossible task I had undertaken but I knew he was there, so he must help me.

Before we retired that evening, I went ahead to secrete my pendulum in my bedside cabinet. I felt rather like a furtive child, not up to any good. I wanted to remain totally undistracted while I considered my intent that evening. It wasn't in any way down to any confidence I had in the pendulum; it would be more a sort of exploratory experiment, a starting block, reacting as I felt to a continuous prompting with logic and rationality totally suspended. I was driven, some may say, by the natural maternal instinct I had, which I cannot deny may well be true; but to consider it at any length would not be helpful in any event.

I thought about the dilemma of savants, the people who present as having severe learning difficulties, or a form of mental affliction stopping them from functioning or performing normally in the world. And yet some of them can demonstrate this extraordinary ability to recall the smallest of detail from any date or time in their past, or to reproduce things on paper after but one glance. Some are able to solve mathematical equations with unquestioningly great accuracy, completely outside the remit of the average individual. The greatest of scientists, great thinkers and mathematicians alike are left completely perplexed by this mystery despite trendy theories. So, is it too far removed from this that an upwelling of fresh insights assaulting the senses is also one of the highest expressions of subjective experience, with its ineffable mysterious promptings?

Alone at last, Clive leaving for his own bed and bidding me good-night as he switched off my lamp. Impatiently, I wait alertly for the otherwise quiet evening to be broken by the slumbering soft snores of Clive in the next room. The familiar sound rising and falling signified the next phase as I quietly put the light back on. Gently I reached for the brass pendulum, raising myself up on the pillows and pulling the quilt around me. The ensuing warmth of my body relaxed me, allowing my mind to meld with the virginal unexplored labyrinth that is my soul.

I raised the chain with my right hand allowing the weight to hang freely over my left hand. I asked Andrew to draw close as I very quietly instructed him in which direction to influence the pendulum. I nominated clockwise for 'yes' and side to side for 'no'. My mind was as one as I focussed intently upon this metal indicator. With pensive expectation, I implored Andrew to make his presence known. The atmosphere felt charged. The pendulum started to move clockwise. I reserved my excitement somewhat as I really was quite unsure whether I was influencing it. There was every chance that I was, instinctively. The air was heavily laden and palpable. My rational self intervened, considering it brutally absurd. Frustrated, I placed this, the projected mode of my possible salvation, back on the bedside table.

• • •

I remained inclined on my pillows, gazing round the room despondently. My subconscious, obviously working away industriously in the far recesses of my mind, allowed an interesting thought to surface. I seized on it, along with my mobile 'phone. I gripped it fiercely, silently shouting into the void, "Please, just tell me you're here! Show me you are here and end this misery of not knowing."

I was aware of EVP (the electronic voice phenomenon). Television had touched on it and I had read about it in various books. Most of the sometimes questionable evidence was quite obscure, bordering in many cases on unintelligible. It was apparent from the remaining voices or sounds caught on recordings that it obviously took a lot of energy, as a word or a small phrase was all that was to be had despite ghost hunters' best efforts. I concluded that to ask Andrew to speak or say anything would be a tall order and would probably end in disappointment. Reflecting on the literature I had read, I supposed that if it was true that spirit energy was electromagnetically based then maybe - just maybe - an interference of an intelligent nature could be creatively forced.

I had also learned that when EVP is attempted and questions asked, the response is not heard at the time but immediately on retrieval, at playback. This is the most curious aspect of EVP as any answers are not within our normal hearing range.

Here goes, I thought. Before I activated the `phone voice recorder, I addressed Andrew as if he were in the room. I asked if he could by some kind of energetic interchange try and communicate with me. I demonstrated, by placing my fingertip on the `phone and tapping twice. "Andrew, if you are there, tap twice like this."

I opened the recorder and said, "Sweetheart, are you there?" I had to assume he was responding, so I continued. There was no set script, I wanted to know if he continued to exist or survive in some way. By the same token, if he was responding as I proceeded, I didn't want answers that may destroy me or have any possibility of doing so. I consciously stayed away from questions such as "Are you happy?" Limited as we would be by 'yes' and 'no' responses, if he had said 'no' I would not be able to bear it. I would then have been more inclined to go to him, whatever that entailed, and to be with him. All I sought to do really was just illuminate the shadows.

Having run out of what I considered to be fairly benign questions, I bade him goodnight and sent him my love and my wishes for him to stay within the love and the light. Having received any response to my communication was secondary; his happiness had always been vicariously mine, united uniquely as only a mother and her child can be.

With trepidation, I started the playback. Oh my God! Almost tearful and euphoric, I heard the solid tap–tap of Andrew's response followed closely by the next one. I could barely breathe, the excitement in the pit of my stomach rising at the enormity of what was occurring. I jumped out of bed, flying through the doors into Clive's room, startling him awake. With a high-pitched barely recognisable voice, scarcely containing myself I cried out, "He's here, Andrew is here! My God." My voice now reduced to little more than an audible whisper, "I can't believe it." I had purposefully placed the ` phone out of my reach during the recording, so I knew it wasn't me - *it was not me!*

Clive, his lamp now on, sat beside me on the bed. I had yet to hear the rest; I wanted him to be in on it. It was too fantastic not to share. The following is an exact transcript of the recording which I have retained and diarised from that time.

*"Sweetheart, are you there?"*

TAP-TAP

*Assuming that Andrew was responding, I said, "Andrew, is that you?"*

TAP-TAP

I decided at this point that it would be better to suggest, *"Tap once for 'yes'."*

TAP

*"And tap twice for 'no', then maybe we can communicate."*

TAP-TAP

*"Are you around, Andrew?"*

TAP-TAP, followed by a distinct and loud single TAP then another TAP.

*"Are you surrounded by love and light?"*

TAP, but then followed by TAP-TAP

*"Are you with my dad?"*

*TAP*

*"Or with your dad's dad?"*

TAP-TAP and then another TAP-TAP

*"Is this world combined with ours?"*

TAP, then TAP-TAP followed by TAP

*"Can you go wherever you want?"*

TAP

*"Do you like the dog?"*

TAP

*"Do you know what I mean about the dog?"*

TAP

*"Do you hear the music?"* (I meant the funeral music I played in the car.)
There was no answer.
*"Do you like the music?"*
TAP
*"Goodnight sweetheart."*

It was an obviously intelligent exchange, accompanied by what would become the familiar background crackling energetic static noise approaching and receding as it interacted with my mobile 'phone voice recorder. Naturally, Clive and I immediately attempted to contact Andrew once more. Whatever energy he'd had was now exhausted as we sat listening to the silent playback, somewhat disappointed. Winning the lottery pales in comparison to what we experienced that night. Andrew had taken this opportunity and, incredibly, proven to me that he lived after death.

Considering the circumstances under which Andrew had passed, I felt the urgent way in which he responded reflected my son; torn between sadness, regret and otherwise. But in some strange way he had been given leave to support me. This was the OK call I had needed!

I went to bed that night drinking my celebratory mug of hot sweet tea and happily reflecting on this final confirmation that was truly a most profound gift. Everyone experiences a potent sense of Aha, and for a brief moment glimpses something that creates an expansive viewpoint. For me, from that moment, I was overwhelmed by an inner calm and wellbeing, an unshakable feeling of immortality accompanied by peace.

Next morning, I felt as though I had slept. I felt warmth, recalling the events of the night before, taking a few minutes for it to make its impression on my memory. If I experienced no more, it would have to remain with me and sustain me for some time to come.

The sun shone as I took the dog for a walk. There were no shadows today as I contemplated the more mystical traditions. These esoteric traditions assume, implicitly or explicitly, that consciousness is fundamental. Scientific tradition explicitly assumes it is secondary. My mind is an incessant wanderer and I now considered something that had always puzzled me. When you dream, you have no recollection of who you are when awake i.e. your day job. Likewise, when awake, the same is true of where you go to when asleep. A famous philosopher by the name of Descartes posed the thought, "Are you awake when you are dreaming or are you dreaming when you are awake?"

These thoughts engaged my mind thoroughly after the previous night. I was always interested in the esoteric rather than the exoteric (institutional) viewpoint. Strangely, not knowing leads to a deep knowing that can't be put into words. Religion can destroy spirituality because it is reliant forever on second-hand opinion – today's flat Earth theory. Ghandi said that "Even if you are in a minority of one, the truth is still the truth." These ideas, though thought-provoking, are not answers but they are a start. I had to open my mind to all possibilities, not to believe what anyone says and retain the right to ask silly questions.

"Hi, Sheila." I answered the 'phone to Andrew's father's wife. She struggled to contain her excitement as she wanted to relate a dream she had experienced the night before, desperately needing to share it with me. Sheila too had been mortally wounded by Andrew's abrupt demise. My instincts, like hers, were to gush in parallel with her the events my experimentation had yielded. But no, I awaited my turn. I wanted to know what prompted this call. Keenly interested, I waited patiently for her unfolding story.

She had dreamed that she was going about her housework, busy with her usual routine. She had noticed a book on the bed, which she was drawn to pick up. As she sat herself on the bed, she placed it on her lap, curious as to the contents of the book. With her left hand, she endeavoured to open it but, startled mid-movement, she was stopped by the sound of Andrew laughing, causing her to look up. Fully aware within her dream, she remonstrated with him. She told him that she didn't know why he was laughing, considering what he had done, and that she didn't consider it to be at all funny.

With this he stopped, indicating the book. He said to her, "You always said you could read me like a book." At this, Sheila's left hand slid slowly down the cover of the book to reveal the title, Andrew Thomas Parton. Then Andrew added, "You shall now have two little birds on your windowsill." This was very personal to Sheila as she always laughed at the little bird that often alighted on her windowsill; she frequently referred to it as being one of her dead relatives whom she had been very fond of. With this encounter, she found herself wide awake and relating it to Andrew's father.

The familiar warmth washed over me, as I assured Sheila that I believed her. I then began to tell her the happenings of last night with barely a pause between my words. This confirmation was her confirmation. She begged to know the details. Where was I? What did Clive think? Happily, I reiterated it all moment by moment, cautious not to omit any detail that would offer us succour. Two souls in unison, trying to grasp the ungraspable. We somehow determined between us that apartness is an illusion of this reality.

# 5
# Beyond Belief

*'Neither a lofty degree of intelligence nor imagination, nor both together, go to the making of genius. Love, love, love, that is the soul of genius.'*

—WOLFGANG AMADEUS MOZART

There is a fine line between madness and sanity, and I hope I'm not crossing it. My contact with Andrew is governed by emotional impulses. I do not profess to have any mediumistic abilities, but I do believe that the sense of ethereal presence and the encompassing feelings that go with it are directed by something intangible, in excess of the five senses, to enable spirit to get its message across. When something occurs through your five senses, like hearing a voice or seeing something move, maybe a fleeting feeling of touch or just a strongly felt embrace of warm presence which you are unable to account for, that is when your departed one is with you. One should seek to create an ambience of possibilities through any channel or mode that spirit energy can employ in its quest to make contact.

If energy is the key, can spirit influence any form of technology? I give this some thought. It's interesting to think of mobile 'phones or emails. If you send an email to the other side of the world and then close your laptop, no-one considers this remotely magical; yet if you go back twenty or thirty years, the very possibility would have sounded preposterous. There was a time before the invention of the microscope when bacteria was a laughable concept. Yet still I question. No scientist of any standing should be allowed to state in whatever fashion, "To our knowledge, it can't happen, therefore it cannot be true." I note the words 'our knowledge', implying this present time. According to past scientists, the Earth was flat or the centre of the universe - there are thousands of such examples. I suppose, in some respects, the problem lies here: if for example you were told, after a lifetime of researching the impact of leeches drawing blood to relieve infection and disease, that new developments undermined your findings and indeed that you were plainly wrong, where would that leave your distinguished career if not in tatters?

Living in the moment as I have become accustomed has meant that few things have missed my attention. Many things of incident in the past would have passed me by without any notice, but now I realise how much I have missed throughout my life by allowing the resident autopilot within me to dally away precious moments of my life. Did I ever really ponder the true beauty of a flower whilst listening to the majestic tones of some awe-inspiring piece of classical music, as the pure medley of sensory vibrations stroked and nurtured my soul? I think not.

What does it for me is that we see the tiniest proportion of visible light. For instance, no-one doubts that infrared or ultraviolet exist even though they are invisible extensions of the colours red and violet - yet people ridicule the paranormal with "What else is there to see, what else is there to hear?" I look at Penny, who hears what I cannot. Another ten, twenty or thirty years down the line, our ancestors will look back at us and scoff at our ignorance, just as we do now.

The 'phone rings, the mellow tones of a lady bringing me back to ground zero again. It is my designated counsellor, duly appointed to make contact with me. I am not particularly impressed or entirely happy to hear from her at this moment. I have been thrashing about for a good deal of time, trying to negotiate my way by whatever means I could. I am abrupt and fairly brusque as I respond to her invitation to see her at the local hospital. This cold reception to her call must have given her pause to wonder how difficult an assignment she would be undertaking. I answer in an offhand, unenthusiastic manner; I have come to expect nothing from any first response services I have encountered and there is just a hint of disdain in my voice. This was fuelled in part by a lifelong bias against counselling. One or two acquaintances I had met during the course of my life frequented counselling services to the point that I considered that it became itself a part of any affliction they had. I don't know why they just didn't come out with "It all went wrong from the point I became an embryo." My attitude and manner is unaltered as I terminate the call, yet with a promise to attend next week at our assigned time and date. For, to my mind, I am on the brink of inviting the support that will suffice and satisfy my hunger.

• • •

I was still struggling with the sale of Andrew's motorbike. I had bought it for him for his birthday in May but had given it to him in March. He had hit the ground running when he left the Navy just over two years ago and had done extremely well. He had secured himself an apartment, fastidiously servicing his bills along with his ever-increasing collection of home comforts and furnishings, catering to his classical tastes. I had bought him the bike to enhance his life and also to make him less reliant on public transport. He could visit us more frequently. From the outset, he was more often out than in, visiting neighbouring villages. He would also make enormous detours on his way to work, which was just behind where he lived, giving him an opportunity to share his pride and joy with his colleagues, constantly updating his stories of where he had been or where he was going that day.

I couldn't bear to look at it now; the whole project had been so exciting. My brother had taken the bike to Birmingham, out of my mind's sight. I couldn't really deal with it for a long time. However, today it was to go to a very honest dealer, the like of which is extremely refreshing, particularly nowadays. Acting as an intermediary, he had managed to obtain for me a cash settlement not too short of what I had paid in the first instance. He'd further enhanced it to obtain some profit for himself; he was more than welcome – he deserved it. As far as I was concerned, he had made a fence out of a skyscraper, for which I owe him my gratitude. Andrew's recently bought helmet and jacket remained in the garage, hidden from view.

I was still intent on further communication with Andrew. The darker the day, the more frequent my attempts. The night after that first contact, I reached out once more to Andrew, to which he had responded strongly; but frustratingly on playback I couldn't make out what I was asking or saying. I always strove to keep my voice down in case I woke Clive, as I liked to be completely undisturbed in the complete silence. Extremely pleasing as this contact was, I was disappointed as I had asked deeper questions but then could not hear anything of what I had said. Still, optimistically I assumed that I had found something very unique. The mobile `phone had always been Andrew's and my more common mode of communication. It had to be, his being so often away in the Navy; however, our bond was such that he would try to call me as soon as he got a signal, furnishing me details of his recent activities. I would see different cultures and countries through his eyes, colourfully brought to life. There was Egypt, Bahrain and many places intermingled with shipboard life and daily routines brought animatedly to life in my mind. It was rather like a serialised ongoing verbal postcard. My mobile was never far from me, forever in reach of my hand, not once missing a call as I loved to hear his voice.

• • •

The day came to go and see the counsellor – great. I was ten minutes early as I parked up, not confident that it would be helpful and not expecting that she was really looking forward to meeting me. I had not so much sounded vulnerable as quite rude, probably considered a bad combination in the trade. I entered the reception with a couple of minutes to go, and leafed through the pamphlets – a colourful list of services for people who were enduring mental health problems.

I was confronted by a very gentle-faced blonde lady, a little smaller than myself, about five foot three. She was slightly older, which pleased me as I grow weary of barely adolescent service providers, newly qualified from the universities of the inexperienced, trying to grasp issues they can't possibly relate to. With broken bones there are obviously set procedures – that's fine. But when you take the quantum leap into mental debility, a certain finesse and creativity is required, rather like playing a game of chess. Every game or person is different. I was led into a room where a student sat with clipboard in hand. My counsellor, Simone, gestured towards a chair next to a table with a huge box of tissues. I felt less guarded with this woman; her instinctive mannerisms and demeanour were faultless and seamless.

With unhurried ease, she offered me a coffee; I accepted and then she sat down opposite me and adjacent to the young student. Did I mind him taking formal notes? I wasn't too concerned unless he attempted to interview me. This wasn't a time to practise counselling. I was curious as to the amount of forms that needed filling in, making me consider that you don't have to go far to know where the rainforest has gone. Most amazing of all, I think on about the eighth or tenth sheet, the nice young man desperately following current protocol asked me if I smoked, to which I asked "Why?" He replied that, if I did, they actually ran a smoking cessation clinic conveniently at this hospital. Almost responding as one afflicted with Tourette's, I retorted "Sod off!" This surprised even me as I had resolved to be polite.

"So," I continued, "let's see, you arrive at the scene of a major pile-up and see someone dreadfully entangled within their vehicle, and having ascertained that they are still breathing you ask, 'Do you smoke?' - followed swiftly by, 'If you do, we run a smoking cessation clinic'. What exactly is the difference? I have just experienced one of the worse episodes that anyone could encounter in their lives, compounded by having lost my second child already, so let's just recap: I don't drink, I don't do drugs and nor am I on medication. So if I want to smoke, or indeed chain-smoke an entire packet, I am not doing too badly!"

He apologised and explained that he had to ask. This exasperated me. "No, you don't have to ask, sometimes exceptions can be made, and just sometimes a dose of common sense would be more suitable." My appointed counsellor interjected "Absolutely" and I liked her more now.

I felt free to talk about Andrew. It freed me from my extracurricular activities, liberating me. I explored the horrific contents of that day and my extreme disappointment at the response of the emergency services, which I had put on hold until recently. I had registered a complaint at a more local police station, although not written; it had been put into the system to be responded to. A couple of 'phone calls had followed and one particular sentence had stood out. Along with apologies the senior officer had continued, in response to my feeling that I had not been taken seriously from the start, that the two officers had been in shock. But yes, they had taken me seriously as all officers would do. I had replied that if they had taken me seriously in the first place, I would not have been the first to find Andrew; and in terms of shock, no-one could have been more shocked than his own mother.

In addressing the complaint, their primary concern was apparent. They didn't want me to go any further. I therefore decided to put it in writing so it couldn't be ignored. Another senior officer was duly assigned to deal with it, and I received a more humane, empathetic response, the only one I had required in the first instance. I had no desire to take it any further. I left it with them to deal with locally, signing away any decision to take it higher. Another one off the list.

I voiced to her my dismay, my dealings with the landlord and his principal desire to keep Andrew's rent paid in advance along with the deposit plus a bill for damage to the door. His once immaculate flat and the remnants of the furniture that he had solicitously put in place had incurred an additional demand – payment for collection of goods. This sat particularly badly with me as I knew that any house-clearing operation would have paid for the many varied furnishings and ornamental items we had left, in our haste to deal with the more momentous issues and fallout around Andrew's act of madness.

I booked an appointment for the following week. Simone put her arms around me; I felt myself stiffen at this contact, having avoided it to date. I made the slow drive home of approximately four miles, playing the music which had accommodatingly become both Andrew's and mine. I affirmed to him that I had received his message loud and clear – I knew that he was there. I pondered the possibilities of exactly where 'there' was. Was he there when I thought of him, or was he kind of always subliminally there? What kind of incorporeal, ethereal existence could it be? I considered the emotional intricacies of this contact, with some due concern for my obsessive tendencies. It had never been enough just to know something or understand something. If something truly interested me, it was rather like an all-consuming impulse to know everything about it, at least until it was satisfactorily concluded within my own mind. If ever there had been a problem in my life, my tendency would be to divert all power and focus to resolving the difficulty. If I was going to embark on this, an impossibility, then I had somehow to reach a kind of compromise with myself. These unusual circumstances provoked this reaction. Anyway it was early days yet, at the moment I could only enjoy it.

I was home. I turned off my continually looping CD.

I looked forward to retiring, as I did every evening. I was forever expecting some response or acknowledgement from Andrew. Any responses I got were all noteworthy for me, though many times I got no answer. There were, however, sometimes more impressive ones which were quite striking. Some may say strange rather than wonderful, but I considered it all somewhat miraculous that a situation like this had come about at all. I continually questioned myself and was forever seeking confirmation.

I asked him on one occasion if it were possible that he could just say a word, hum a tune or whistle. With thanks to recording technology, and as God is my witness, Andrew whistled directly after the word whistle. How can I describe or quantify how that feels? His whistle was pronounced and tuneful. In that moment, it was not a whistle just for me, it was for anyone who had lost anybody they had been devoted to. I put my mobile down, thoroughly contented in the knowledge that I had not lost the plot.

Yes, I know that the mind is an enormously powerful unknown in itself. But to my knowledge it has never been able to whistle on record, and neither has it ever been known audibly to respond. I never pre-empted responses, always wondering what they would be, sometimes surprised and often a little puzzled; but nevertheless there were intelligent responses. My recordings never amounted to any more than thirty to forty seconds' worth on the recorder, but it appeared to be enough. Many times I got nothing, but when they did come they were obvious. They certainly were not as loud as they had been on the first few occasions, but they were very discernible and evidently Andrew, accompanied invariably by warm sentient feelings.

Sometimes I got answers to one or two questions, and sometimes there were no answers, overridden by a form of mutually agreed code that Andrew could convey by way of some kind of energetic interchange with the voice recorder. His resultant efforts manifested in an audible, electrical relaying of his answers. One tap would indicate 'yes', two taps would indicate 'no' and three taps would assuredly be to send his love during exchanges with me. Talking into the dark silence of my room, it felt almost like a form of communion. Assuming that I too was composed essentially of energy, I reached out, imagining my own energetic field entangling with his to facilitate our communication. This was followed by my replaying the recorder, excited by the prospect of having captured another swift exchange. If I had, the lamp would go off as I slipped down into the warmth of my duvet with a bittersweet smile, contented in some small way that Andrew was indeed still here.

After every effort to contact Andrew, I always closed by sending prayers and blessings for all I knew who had passed. I felt responsible in some way, because of Andrew's transition. I urged him to stay with the love and the light, never once addressing his reasons or decision to leave us, and neither did I ever speak in anger. There was nothing I could do to alter what had happened, but I could reinforce my love and it could be returned. As I drifted off to sleep, I would invite Andrew to stay with me subliminally and, for now, just be there for me.

• • •

There is a limit to what I can ask. I have accumulated many recordings; I really must download them to the computer in case my 'phone breaks, stops working or I damage it. I skirt around and stay away from the one question I will not ask, which is "Are you happy?" I could not bear it if he answered 'no', because I could not go to him. My hunger is such that I need more as I settle down again this evening. Clive has retired, my lamp is now on, I place my 'phone within the receivable distance of my whispered requests...

As Clive brings in my rejuvenating mug of caffeine elixir next day, I tell him about the recent outcomes of my continuing experiments. I have noticed it before, but it is becoming more frequent now. I have convinced myself that Andrews's energy is drawing closer, this being indicated by the increasing strength of the static, energetic build-up emanating from my recorder on playback. The affiliated feelings with it are a little uncomfortable, but I feel that maybe by persevering I am on the edge of some kind of breakthrough. The feeling accompanying the energy seems to permeate the right side of my body entirely, causing an unsettled reaction in me. A cold tingly sensation responds to this presence, but I put this down to my inexperience of feeling or detecting presence.

I have identified this noise before, very much in the background of Andrew and my interaction. But this noise is quite loud marking it out as very different; again, I still put this down to Andrew drawing closer. I invite Clive to listen to it, he raises his eyebrows remarking that it is unusual; ever confident at the time that it brings the relief I seek, he concurs with me.

Since the whistle incident, I have felt that communication with Andrew is getting more difficult, half of me thinking that maybe he is in the process of moving on or allowing me to. On the other hand, with the energy noise building, something still makes me suspect that something is about to happen. I am impatient for it.

Today, I have to collect Andrew's ashes. I park up by the crematorium; it's a bright sunny day with just a hint of wind, blowing the forlorn petals of the abandoned blooms left reverently behind by the unfortunate visitors to the chapel. I take in the modern building adjacent to the saddest of venues. It's a straight path to the door. Fixing my gaze ahead, glancing neither right nor left, I walk the thirty feet. There is no-one about as I enter the brightly lit reception area, with glass cases of decorative urns of varying sizes, designs and of course prices. A smartly dressed young man arrives at the reception desk; I address him sombrely, requesting my son's ashes. I just want to get this over with as he shows me an adjoining room, nicely decorated with two chairs and a coffee table. I seat myself, awaiting the arrival of the decimated remains of my son.

He unties the red velvet bag revealing the golden plastic urn with Andrew's name printed upon it. It's so bizarre; I can barely take it in, as he re-ties the checked contents and slides the container towards me. I pick the precious package up tenderly, holding it closely to me as I would have once held Andrew as a baby. Now words defeat me, I cannot trust myself to speak; I must just get to the car. I walk as quickly as I can, I don't want to attract attention as the tears blur my eyes, but it is obvious as one or two people now parking up show. A noisy child is taken in hand, as first the mother looks at me and then her gaze drops to the ground. Another adult stands aside as I stride past him, his head bowed. I get into the car, placing Andrews's ashes on the passenger seat securely. I voice some memories aloud as though his spirit is present, talking of the times when I had picked him up from the train station when he had come home on leave, the day trips we had shared in the car. In fact, the last time he had been in the car we had all gone to Warwick Castle on a day trip the Wednesday before he passed.

"Oh, Andrew, what have you done?"

As I enter the driveway, I feel the familiar peace and calm drift over me, reinforced by the memory of that first contact and his seemingly desperate pronounced energetic taps on my recorder. I place him in the wardrobe of his once bedroom, gently closing the wardrobe doors. I really do need a coffee.

I stand in the garden going through some of the recordings I have gathered, bittersweet and yet under the circumstances extremely comforting. I return to the house, passing the small patch of aggravated concrete where Andrew had hastily kicked down his bike stand on his many visits to us. I hope they never disappear, these last physical traces.

Wearily I retire to bed once more, again waiting patiently for Clive to retire. The lamp goes on, I reach for my mobile. I know something is there because I can hear the loud ebb and flow of the energetic noise; I just wish it would break and reveal itself, as I expectantly thought it might. The lamp goes off and I turn over. I offer up my nightly prayer, that Andrew and Adam and anyone I know who had passed remain together in the love and light, or wherever it is we are led to believe in.

I ask Andrew that if he is having difficulty communicating, could I visit him? I remember vividly the lucid dream that followed. I found myself in the back of an Army lorry, with no windows. This didn't seem particularly odd at the time as I had been in the Army, and travelling in the rear of a four-tonner was not unusual. I asked the faceless driver where he was going to drop me off, and he told me to wait and see.

The vehicle stopped, the back opened for me to jump down from. I didn't ever see the face of the driver, communicating by way of asides. I asked him what I was to do there, to which he replied that I should just go for a wander. I enquired what time he would collect me – he didn't answer. I found myself in some sort of small town, nothing remarkable although it was completely pedestrianised. I looked round for places that attracted my interest. I saw a carpet shop and I made my way towards it. As I entered, a kindly man came towards me with an enquiring face as I told him I was looking for a rug for my son's bedroom, but as he had died it would not be for heavy use; maybe a red one. With this he sat down, inviting me to sit with him and tell my story and the sorry circumstance. I liked him very much, thanked him for his time and left the shop without a rug.

From the doorway, further along to the left I saw a gazebo made of canvass. This was the first sign of life I had seen as I meandered towards it. As I drew nearer, I noticed a dark-haired, middle-aged lady with glasses and a clip board, standing in front of a whiteboard opposite three offset leather two-seater settees. Her eyes were lit up from within, a smile as though she knew me which momentarily caused me to try and recollect who she was. She closed in on me, leaning slightly towards me as she did. "Andrew will be with you in a moment." Smiling, she continued, "You know, his face was soaking wet when we found him." I was speechless, incredulous; I looked at her as though I had misheard.

I had not heard that expression before, but I had taken it at the time that, yes, he had indeed been found and collected. She invited me to sit down, gesturing towards one of the small leather sofas. Andrew came from behind me, reaching out seemingly to make contact with my shoulder as he swept past from behind. As he did so he said, "I'm sorry, Mum, I am so sorry." Walking towards the end of the sofa he stopped and turned towards me, his hand immediately rising to his throat, drawing my attention to a black diffused line running down from the bottom of his chin and extending downwardly towards his collarbone. I thought this strange because I knew he had hanged himself, but this line was running downwards.

Stroking his throat, he said, "I cannot stay long because, as you can see, my voice is weak." Once again, I knew that his energy was such that any time was limited. I arose and walked unbelieving towards him. He was wearing an almost luminescent suit of silvery grey, although he had been buried in a dark suit and tie. His face was pale and yet devoid of the small somewhat trendy goatee beard he had been nurturing, and his hair was longer. I could barely believe it, but in those poignant seconds that followed I knew he was not dead in every sense of the word.

Understanding so much at that time, I struggled under pressure to formulate some questions that would satisfy my yearnings for some time to come. I said to him, "Can you see me all the time?"

He responded, "Yes, but I don't."

I followed up with my next and asked, "Those books I have read, are they true?"

Andrew replied, "Yes, they are."

I then asked him, "What is there is to do here?" as I looked around.

He responded, "There is lots to do, a lot to do."

I then enquired of him that if, say, he wanted to play the guitar, "Do you just think of it?"

He looked at me in the familiar way that only Andrew did, implying "Pretty much."

With that, I saw his form dissolving into the rapidly encroaching darkness that descended. I knew that my time with him was at a close for now.

My eyes flit open; I am back within the confines of my bedroom, utterly convinced that I have visited him. I thank him profusely, along with any facilitating guides, whatever or whoever had assisted this reunion. Contentedly, I once more roll over.

# 6
## Warning Shot!

'Man's mind, stretched to a new idea,
never goes back to its original dimensions.'

—Oliver Wendell Holmes

I'm feeling brighter lately. A newly found confidence has entered the stage. With the books that are now encroaching on most of my bedroom, my once strong durable bookcase is now beginning to bend and bow towards the centres of the shelves.

I draw on different aspects of the varying hypotheses of opinion - some based purely on the spiritual, others are the cutting edge of science, giving rise in my mind to the increasing unification of the two. It strikes me that most of the interesting research and the more important potential outcomes or conclusions (outside parapsychology) is carried out by retired professors or established academic authors. This makes me question the in-post academics' inability to explore what in the mainstream are considered fringe concepts. But our governing masters decree the educational diet of the current dogma, giving little room for 'paradigm shifts'.

I have been unable to resist telling some of my clients that I knew Andrew was ok because I had contacted him. Many had queried why I was still walking. Some of them looked at me in the way you observe someone who is badly deluded, but others now enquire if I have heard from Andrew lately – waiting with bated breath for the next instalment.

One of my more frequent experiences is their very human tendency to express that almost thoughtless response "It would kill me!" and other such reactions. Do they think that I, for one moment before the fact, could have envisioned living with it? I wonder if by negotiating my way in the only way I could, I had somehow let collective motherhood down. I muse that if I somehow climbed upon some sort of metaphoric funeral pyre, I would exonerate myself of my failure to grieve appropriately, acquitting myself with excellence in mothering credentials. They could then stand back with mutual approval as "It was only to be expected because, as we all know, no mother could live with that."

My normal routine has resumed now. I arise at eight o'clock in the morning. I have more focus than I had because I now have a project. I look in the mirror, the pallor I had has abated and I look healthy. The reflection is appraised by sad blue eyes; I lift my eyebrows along with my lids consciously, in remembrance of how they used to look. Raising my forehead against its apparent tendency to frown, I realise I have to make an effort in that department. I don't want people to know from the way I look or comport myself the catastrophe I have experienced. For some reason, I find their sympathy debilitating, it weakens me. If on the other hand people interact with me normally, I find that affirming and strengthening. I sometimes pass my more intimate feelings to Clive who awaits these opportunities, always taking the time to stop what he is doing. It is enough for me, rather akin to someone banging you on your back when you have a piece of meat stuck, your throat then cleared and away you go. My autopilot is nearly redundant; my word, what a capable fellow it was. It is comforting to know it is still available as and when I require it. With my mirror fascinations at an end, I go to make a cup of coffee.

I remember that I have to go and ring my brother, sliding my mobile open to make the call only to find Andrew's number displayed. "Strange," I think fleetingly, as I thumb through the numbers. I continue with the day's schedule. Sometimes, when I take a longer lunch than I normally do, I will open my `phone recorder, listening to past recordings. I think one of the reasons I persist in revisiting my recent attempts is because I am quite a critical thinker, forever analysing. I consider all sorts of hypotheses, even becoming quite methodical in my efforts. I try to eradicate any possible background influences, try to replicate accidental noises purposefully myself; but no, it's not the same at all. I do this as I am keen to satisfy myself to the best of my ability that I am not fooling myself. In addition to the audible responses, I notice the silence as I speak and the apparent answers resounding appropriately.

I know that people are aware from their relatives and friends who have lost children, parents, husbands etcetera, that contact does occur. But this is often denied in a somewhat patronising manner. They tell you it is quite normal to sense the survival of your loved one and, if pushed, they go into some sort of explanation as to how grief can impact and influence the mind. This is interesting when you consider that they know nothing about the mind. Psychiatry could almost be considered a pseudoscience, extremely subjective. The huge index of mental health problems gets bigger by the year, forever being updated. I do not deny that mental health conditions exist; however, I deny people the right to tell others uniformly that they are imagining things. Yes, they would say it is quite normal and I would say it is exceedingly normal, considering my experiences. Many of my clients have conveyed stories to me which in the past I would have nodded sympathetically at, but now I tell them, "I believe you."

Experiments in quantum physics appear to indicate that 'believing is seeing' and not 'seeing is believing'. Mainstream science has never tackled consciousness. They don't even know where our memories are stored. In the paradigm that they work with, taking consciousness into consideration is a profound flaw. Basically, it is the desire to stem people's feelings and deep intuition that does the most damage.

• • •

It's Sunday today, a few days short of my birthday, and I do wonder if I will hear from Andrew. Sometimes, when I access my `phone, I still see his number displayed, prompting me to ensure the screen is shut when I close it. I don't want to obscure the experiences further by any fallibility on my part.

Clive and I are going to a garden centre, although we don't really want to buy anything. We tend just to go and look around. I do love plants and flowers and I have quite a variety scattered about the house. They generally end up on life support, swiftly followed up by the intensive care team which is Clive, who encouragingly strokes their leaves. I do try and they aren't short of love and attention, but perhaps my lack of success is down to too much love and attention resulting in overkill. I get the feeling that when I go into commercial garden centres to acquire my target plant, I hear the faint shuffling of pots as they edge to the back of the shelf. I almost imagine the soft murmuring of the plants talking amongst themselves and alluding to me, that if my gaze should fall upon them they are doomed. This never halted my sadistic tendencies, though, as I grasped the next unfortunate victim.

We always have a coffee when we are out, which currently promotes quite a depth of conversation on the metaphysical. We are both of us awed by what has happened. We both find ourselves catapulted from the more classical worldview invariably into the more mysterious. It was perhaps less immediate than for some, because we had always questioned the fabric of reality. But like most people, unless you had experienced it irrevocably yourself first hand, you are largely reliant on other people's opinions.

Today's hot topic is the frequency of Andrew's name appearing on my `phone, and likewise on Sheila's. I ask him if he has experienced it and he says not. Diversifying a little, Clive suggests that I might ask Andrew for a text. Laughingly, I respond that I have already asked Andrew to interfere with his `phone; but to expect a text, I continue humorously, would I think be beyond Andrew's abilities. Nevertheless, you can live in hope.

The next day, Monday, another boring day at the office so to speak, Clive greets me as I enter the house. He tells me I would never guess what had happened to him that day. He had been at his computer when he had received an automated text from Andrew's Facebook page, encouragingly saying, "Andrew accepts Clive as a friend." I sit down, absolutely stunned and amazed. I can't believe what I am hearing, that maybe Andrew had overheard our conversation of yesterday.

Andrew's Facebook page had been completely inaccessible since he died. He was the only one who could access it, unless we forward a death certificate to Facebook Accounts to remove it. I had decided against this, allowing it to stand for what I know from those who interacted with it that it had attracted a long list of thoughts and condolences along with memories. Clive and I do not have Facebook pages and never communicated with him through Facebook. So once more the rational gave way to the strange.

I am keen to catch up with Sheila, calling to arrange a suitable time for a visit. I want to let her hear the recordings that I had told her about. She tells me she believes me but I can't wait for her to have the opportunity to hear them herself. The additional 'friend acceptance' from Andrew's Facebook page was like the icing on the cake. It's my birthday in a few days' time and I shall see her the day after. The thought of this prompts me to consider that I haven't received anything remotely symbolic from Andrew. I didn't know how it would manifest, maybe the late flowering of a rose or possibly one of my dying plants springing to life. I didn't really know, although I half thought it to be a ludicrous expectation. It wouldn't faze me if didn't receive anything, but nevertheless…

I have Andrews's landline 'phone with answerphone stored. I take it out for the first time and methodically plug it in. There it is, Andrew's voice, a not too distant echo from the past. "Hi, it's Andrew, I'm not able to take your call at the moment, but if you would like to leave your name and number I will call you back." It has hollowness about it, the same hollowness I detected that day he left us. I perceive it differently now; I hated leaving messages, I only ever left one that day I sped over to Buxton. I play it several times before dismantling it, resealing it in the bag I keep it in. I place it back under my bed.

• • •

I still have his ashes, still in the wardrobe, and I don't want them moved. I have decided our ashes will be merged when it is my turn. As together in life, so shall we be at the end.

Returning home in the evening, I drew into the driveway with an almost self-satisfied smile on my face. Driving home as normal, my eyes had been continually drawn to the battered Asda carrier bag placed on the passenger seat. The exterior of the bag betrayed the presence of that within, a spray of colourful flower heads peeking out of the top. I had no sooner finished with one particular client than she had arisen and gone into her adjacent lounge, appearing once more in the kitchen with a bunch of flowers she had retrieved from her own vase in the window, wordlessly placing these splendid blooms into this tired supermarket bag. Simultaneously, she motioned for me to take them from her. I looked at her questioningly, as she said, "I felt I needed to give these to you." I thanked her profusely for this gesture, no longer amazed, but more with a feeling of inner awe.

I pulled on my handbrake, purposefully walking through the house to the kitchen to find an appropriate vase. My vase of flowers now sat resplendent next to my birthday cards. "Thank you, Andrew."

I couldn't wait to tell Sheila and Alex as I sped over the hills later. The requested painting by Andrew sat on the back seat, a painting of an ex-girlfriend that he had captured lovingly on canvas. His attention to detail was impeccable, and although colour blind he still managed to capture an essence of luminosity which trademarked his efforts and abilities.

Eagerly I waited in excited anticipation for the door of the flats complex to beckon entrance. This was the first time that anybody apart from Clive had had the opportunity to marvel at what I had captured on record. Sheila in particular was very keen to hear it as she had always been spiritually minded. A very kind and gentle lady, she had extended this gentleness to Andrew in a maternal fashion. Andrew's dad, on the other hand, was perturbed by the whole business, not at all believing in the more mystical religious traditions. However, when I selected the sound bite of Andrew seemingly responding to a requested whistle, he threw back his head laughing, his eyes briefly gleeful. "Yes, I heard it," he exclaimed. Sheila and I engaged in conversation about other possible signs we had encountered. As we did, I commented as to whether or not Andrew might be in attendance with us.

Almost playfully, in the good humour of the moment, I brought out my 'phone to attempt contact Andrew. It drew a negative, but we had to try. During the course of my visit, the home landline had rung twice but Sheila had chosen to ignore it in light of the conversation we were having. Still, the time came when I had to leave, having had about three cups of coffee. Alex was accompanying me to the front door when Sheila shouted excitedly for me to return quickly. Pushing her home 'phone towards me, she asked me to identify the caller number displayed. The number was their own, having called twice. Good grief!

## 28th October, 2011

It was lunchtime as I pulled in, as I regularly do, for a cappuccino from the McDonald's drive-thru.

I was eager to go through my recordings to date, to add to those presently piling up on the hard drive of the computer at home. I was keen to download them in the main for three reasons, the first being that I would have an indelible record of my communications to date, the second was to capture it all for posterity in case I lost my 'phone, broke it or it just packed in. I was conscious that it was getting 'tired', indicated by its tendency to shut off mid-recording. The third reason was so that I could hear the recordings through the amplified speakers, dipping and delving at leisure.

I marked these recordings in the back of my work diary, according each and every one with remarks on what I heard. I left an occasional base line in. I have captured the strange build-up of static I have been getting and, of course, my attempted discourse with Andrew via tapping and his more tuneful interludes. I deleted the ones of little interest. The job completed, I was on my way.

Having dinner that evening with Clive, I was impatient to download my more recent cachet. I served coffee, I fed the dog.

I looked on as Clive attended to the cable connection between the mobile and the computer, then we were off. Clive now appraised through the speakers with fresh ears the intelligence of the responses. And yes, there were defined tunes as we heard the drumming. I told him I would like to hear a couple more, the ones with that strange almost imposing sound of energetic static - the rise and fall strikingly reminiscent of the noise a plasma ball makes, which we have observed in laboratories.

The static I expected was interrupted suddenly by a huge 'rap' similar to the crack of a whip or leather belt, followed by two or three more in quick succession. Then a vacuum-like stillness with just a hint of snapping and popping in the background. Then a voice, clear as a bell. With little intonation but such clarity, it was bone-chilling: "Chockas wait in the night." Just that!

There was no mistaking the content of the sentence; in fact, it was almost unreasonably clear under the circumstances. Clive spluttered as he turned to me, my mouth agape, and demanded, "What the hell was that?"

I was completely shell shocked. I stood up before he replayed it, on my way to make coffee, retreating from the room hastily. I heard him from the confines of the kitchen playing and replaying it. I returned with two cups in hand. He then remonstrated with me, telling me I was running around like an ice cream wagon, attracting goodness knows what. Stunned, I countered that this recording had not been there this afternoon. I had been doing it so regularly that I would have come across it sooner on playback and desisted from this activity.

The recording was two weeks old. That voice had transposed itself onto an existing recording between lunchtime and this evening

Clive told me that I need to stop doing this and readily I agreed with him. How in the name of God that recording appeared defeated me entirely. I was very frightened; I had not considered the implications of what I was doing. However, the enormity of knowing for sure, in that moment, that there was definitely another dimension of life answered the biggest of all questions as far as I was concerned!

It was a dark winter's night as I illuminated the entire house. The home that I had once considered both a refuge and respite from the troubled world outside its windows became a place of immediate alarm. Within the invisible realms of dark matter, which we cannot perceive, dwelt a force far above my heavenly imaginings. My eyes now darted about me - unknown territory indeed.

My researches into science and spirituality could not help me now; in fact, faced with this stark fearsome occurrence, I was at a loss as to what could help me now. I felt for the absolutely first time that I had been thoroughly slapped in the face by the unimaginable. The sad fact was that no-one would believe me. Clive resolutely assured me that I was to remember that mischievous spirits pass alongside the virtuous.

This in no way detracted from my feelings of vulnerability in any way. I decided that this night I would sleep with the light on.

I pondered this contradiction, as I obviously could not see it even with the lights on. I demanded of my relatives who had passed over that they fend off this uninvited guest. Yet, although frightened, inwardly I pondered the more fantastic implications. I had never doubted my contact with Andrew, but had I fooled myself in any way? This was undeniably the final confirmation that there is indeed another dimension of which we are not aware.

My whole intense focus over the last few months was on trying to communicate with my son. The time and the energy I had expended had drawn something untoward from the void of my expectation. Whatever it was, its energy was stronger than Andrew's. I had been monitoring it and its incremental energy building up over the last few weeks. I had assumed all along that it had been Andrew. I was so wrong!

Clive put on a brave face, but I could tell from the subtleties of his body language that he was not at all unaffected. He tapped 'chokas' into the computer, with variations on the spelling. Outside of chocolate sundaes and fluffy boots, there were only a few other references, excerpts from and commentaries on the Jewish Torah (for example, Numbers 9:10). Grasping at straws, we selected one or two links. Earnestly, our eyes scanned downwardly, seeking maybe some kind of clue or anything that bore any correlation to what we had both experienced. As far as we could understand it, the word refers to 'one who is distant'; it has a double meaning, the first being 'far from a place' and the second being 'spiritually impure' or 'defiled'. The implications of the latter hardly bore thinking about.

Was this message suggesting that 'those who are far away (in another life) can be reached in the night' or, more threateningly, that 'dark spirits are waiting to contact us'?

It was enough for Clive, and he downloaded all recordings to disk whilst I also deleted everything I had on my mobile except my very special first contact. Disk in hand, Clive passed me purposefully, focussed on depositing the recordings amongst Andrew's belongings in the garage.

That night it was not easily dismissed because, whatever the take on it, to me it felt like a warning - a warning shot!

Now, I had to go to bed, I had to be up tomorrow. Happy, I was not. I found the lamp in my bedroom not conducive to sleep. We experimented with drapes, books and paper, attempting to subdue the lamp's glare, then reluctantly letting it be, cautious of fire hazard. I turned to the wall to shield me from the brightness, but then felt compelled to turn once more, should I be sneaked up on. I felt somewhat like a child, clutching the cross around my neck tightly, apologising to the powers-that-be for my persistence. It was not a good night and I was grateful for the morning light.

I thought long and hard next morning about the consequences of the night before. Although still very frightening, it was almost worth the price because I had captured something far and above any expectation. This had exonerated me of any imagination, totally, completely and absolutely. It was abundantly clear that something could permeate our plane of existence; the other striking and remarkable fact is that whatever it was could operate outside of time. I had listened to those recordings as another person would dose on a tonic.

I reflected on the notes made in the back of my work diary: "Strong energy noise." Once a recording was made on that Samsung `phone recorder, the file could not be re-used, only deleted and then superseded by a successive recording. I lived the remainder of that day with a mixture of both awe and fear.

Clive was now concerned about what he considered to be an unhealthy pursuit, for clearly I had less control than I had thought. However, I could not help feeling a little clever at having had this verification of the unknown. Who would know about these things? It could wait, because for now my attention was focussed on how I was going to sleep at night.

In my less frantic moments, I reflected on the noise of the energy before the voice transposed itself over it, the rise and fall of this energy like noise I had become familiar with since my first contact. I could detect it on many of the communications I had had with Andrew; however, on those occasions it had been far more subtle. This sound had become far more imposing over the last few weeks and, in my misguided excitement, I had supposed that Andrew was drawing nearer. I thought back and deliberated on the difference between the contrasting energy sounds. Andrew always came through with a warmth and knowing; on the other hand, the stronger energy had made me feel uncomfortable, accompanied by a strange tingling down my side. I had just thought that maybe Andrew was about to manifest more strongly.

The energy is a most intriguing area in itself for me. We are surrounded by an energy field and we are energy beings. We get our energy from this field and everything, including ourselves, is made up of energy, vibrating at specific frequencies.

"There is no place in this new kind of physics both for the field and matter, for the field is the only reality," said Albert Einstein. Quantum physics reveals the universe to be a gigantic field of energy, in which matter is just a slowed down form of energy.

There is now a growing body of renegade scientists who have ventured into the domain of the spiritual in an attempt to interpret the inexplicable findings of some experiments. Scientists such as Dr Rupert Sheldrake, Dr Stuart Hameroff and Sir Roger Penrose. Science is now discovering what eastern mystics have always known: shamans and mystics refer to this field of energy as a "oneness" and an interconnectedness.

For now, my desire was only to merge peacefully with my pillow and sleep through, leaving any further rumination for those of us who are awake...

# 7
# Lighting Up the Darkness

'I have never seen a monument erected to a pessimist.'
—Paul Harvey

Christmas was coming. This was a particular dark period for me, compounded by the shock of my unknown visitor making contact. I reactivated my autopilot as I tenaciously re-enforced my imaginary barricades. I had adopted this ability to blank Christmas entirely from my mind, and this also extended strangely to the daily exchanges with people as soon as Christmas was introduced into the conversation. I realised that Christmas was not on hold for everybody and in fact, for many, Christmas is the highlight of the year; a time for family, the exchange of presents and warm feelings. I listened animatedly, allowing none of it to leave its impression on my mind as it passed through me. Unfortunately, I also realised later that this impacted on Clive indirectly.

Clive's birthday is in December, a little before the celebrated day. I was so well practised that no matter how subtle the hints of his approaching birthday, it had been blanked from my mind entirely. So keen was I to avoid the term 'Christmas', this had also transmuted to encompass the word 'birthday'. The day came, and Clive was a little more despondent than normal - I assumed that the year was taking its toll. I noticed that a card appeared on the mantelpiece and I automatically assumed that he had placed a dated Christmas card there in celebration of past years when his parents had been here. This prompted me to consider bringing out one of Andrew's old cards.

Kneeling on the floor with an assortment of cards through the ages, like the cards I had found kept and bound amongst Andrew's possessions still in the garage, I picked up one and then another, getting lost within the echoes of the reciprocated sentiments. The words now reverberated with hollow intensity. I returned them to the drawer. When Clive returned from work, I complimented him on placing the old Christmas card on the mantelpiece. I told him of my attempts to do the same for Andrew, but hadn't felt it such a good idea. Disbelievingly, I was staggered to learn that the card had been a birthday card from a mutual friend of ours. I had missed it entirely.

I immediately recollected various earlier comments, filling in the blanks. Although this omission had upset him, understandably, it hadn't been by conscious design. I could not make up this ground and neither did he expect it; I would make it up to him at a later date, for his patience and tenacious support.

• • •

I still longed to resume contact with Andrew, but after the events of late I must admit I was fearful. Clive and I had to go purposefully to town to purchase a small night light, something sufficiently dim to facilitate sleep but one that could illuminate the darkest corners of my room.

I beseeched the forces of light to gather about me, addressing my concerns directly to any angelic beings and guardian spirits. I apologised for any impropriety on my part, if I had been too persistent and intercepted by who knows what. I was comforted by thoughts of those whom I have loved and gone before me, and who would have my interests at heart. I also asked them to draw closer to me. Clive would tell me that there are bad people this side of life and they too pass on, so we cannot assume that their characteristics do not also pass on. At the moment, this didn't help as I scanned my room. I woke periodically throughout the night, like a child with a waking nightmare, pulling the quilt up and ever tighter round me. It was difficult to sleep with the light on but, unfortunately, more difficult with the light off. Unusually, I switched both my mobiles off, considering that maybe spirits can traverse the various invisible signals. My own 'phone was presently acting like a homing beacon, instead of a candle for my beloved son.

The autopilot was not very useful to me at this time, as it required absolute vigilance. With just over a week to go before Christmas, I was kept busied by my usual routines.

I passed an upturned photograph frame in the window of the lounge. I had laid it flat from the day that Andrew had passed. My gaze fixed on it as I drew towards it and with a little hesitation I moved to right the frame as it had formerly stood, in pride of place. There was Andrew's image with Clive, proudly standing there in his naval uniform on the day he had passed out into the Royal Navy. I remembered that day very well, vividly emblazoned in my memory. I had been so excited, alongside his pride in his achievement, and how well he had looked in the July sunshine. I remembered, as they had marched onto the parade square accompanied by the Royal Marine band, a lump forming in my throat. I had struggled to contain the surge of emotion that had encompassed me, overwhelmed with happiness overseeing this, the transition of my son from boyhood to man. I had hugged him tightly to me just before this photo had been taken. Almost giddily, I had looked on as a formal photograph had been taken, a much larger and imposing one which I had placed in the dining room, where it remains to this day. It now had the additional feature of Andrew's golden cross that he had worn continually, attached to the frame of the picture. The smaller photograph was now upright in its frame, looking once again inwardly onto the lounge.

I made my mind up to approach the church; as I was not sleeping too well, I knew that at least there they would accept it unquestioningly. I was not in the mood for having my credibility doubted in any way. I called in on the rectory on the way back from work, but the vicar was not at home.

But on arrival at home, by strange coincidence, a lady from the church, a local lay pastor who had been visiting quite frequently, was sat on the settee. Although Clive would never admit it, my belief was that he had sought her out himself and asked her to arrive 'unexpectedly'. I let this subterfuge pass. He did not know that I had attempted overtures myself. There was little hesitation as I related to her the exercise of that evening. Her eyes betrayed volumes as her face remained unchanged, unblinking as I related my story. A pregnant pause, and then she invited me to pray with her.

I told her that I had rather hoped she would, by way of the light of her untarnished spirit, clear the house for us. I felt that the prayers of her empowered soul and belief would somehow make up for my enfeebled spirit at that time. I don't know if she had come across this before but, if she had ever heard of it, she gave nothing away. I found her faith reassuring, I felt confident of her pure intention to clear the house and that my belief in that would assist her. Self-assuredly, she arose and went from room to room, with me following close behind her. She spoke in tongues, which I believe have a Pentecostal origin. From research I had done to date, this didn't perturb me in the slightest. I had concluded that in the absence of adequate words, pure love and the consciousness of intention is the all-consuming power, assisted ably by my surrendering at that moment, calling on the symbolic supremacy of protection and enlightenment. I have to admit that in the absence of knowing who or what or where the voice came from, words cannot fail to defeat you.

"Oh Andrew, what have you done that I have to resort to this?"

I thanked her profusely as we united in a final prayer. At that moment in time, this was the best I could do. Short of running the risk of being sectioned, it was certainly the safest, I inwardly mused. As I bade her goodbye at the door, I vowed to myself that I would not do it again. But, rather like a doomed alcoholic or drug addict, I further considered… just once more, but not yet.

Clive turned to me, reminding me that I have had more than enough contact with Andrew, more than enough evidence, and that Andrew would get in contact with me if it was needed. He told me that I should no longer pursue it. I kept my counsel, I could say nothing. All through Andrew's adulthood, even when he was away with the Navy, we had spoken daily. I had embraced this continuation of contact and so could not trust myself long term. Contact with my son had ultimately been responsible for my maintaining my own health, both physically and mentally, by constantly seeking reassurance of his continued existence.

LIGHTING UP THE DARKNESS

Right now it was easy to desist, as fear is a great enabler; and, although I would try, I could promise nothing. I rather felt like that character in Close Encounters Of The Third Kind, his obsession with alien contact having been brought about by an encounter with a UFO in the first part of the film. He was only exonerated of his highly questionable compulsion towards the close, when invited to join the others as the incredulous eyes of the observers looked on. I was conscious of this and its impact on those I had chosen to disclose to on occasion.

• • •

I exercise far more control lately. It is a difficult concept to grapple with, when taken from cold. I also have to bear in mind my relationship with Clive and the influences this entire year has brought to bear and its residual impressions. I go and make a coffee.

The world looks very different today, as I contemplate my mirror image. I brush my teeth, ever watchful of the reflection behind me. I am frustrated by my physical limitations and I lament classical science's blinkered overview in which we live. Shut away in their partially sighted academic cloisters, they would not entertain someone like me. How could I start to convey what happened, when far more qualified and educated minds than mine have struggled with the establishment?

It is one of my darker evenings as I retire, after ensuring that both my mobiles are switched off. I implore Andrew, and only Andrew, I am very specific. In light of the apparent birthday response of 'flowers', I ask him if it is at all possible, by way of a sort of challenge or confirmation, that he could procure a Christmas present for me. Following this with my normal wishes and prayers that he stays with the love and light, I turn over.

The priority for today is that I need to purchase a Demon lamp. Unconvinced as I am that having a light on in the bedroom makes a difference, it satisfies my physical senses. I need a light with a more subdued affect, more conducive to sleep. I opt for a full faux suede lantern; this is satisfying on two fronts, the first being that it completely encloses the low wattage bulb. The second and most attractive of its features is that it has butterfly silhouettes cut out of the fabric shade, allowing a happy projection of these freedom-loving beings of nature.

The next night I settle, scanning the room, counting each and every luminous butterfly. I count the big ones and then I count the small ones. Eventually, as weary as one could be of counting sheep, I close my eyes still ever alert to an odd noise or creak. I must admit, I still find it difficult to sleep, rising once or twice in the night. I go downstairs to make a cup of tea and let the dog out as she is always keen. I look up at the moon and identify as many constellations as I can. Our ancestors knew something in the absence of technology. What insights have we lost in just a few thousand years, what knowledge have we forsaken or misplaced by our words and translations and indeed our arrogance? I marvel at the philosophers of ancient Greece, as their contemplations appear to be gaining ground in science. "Incredible," I think, as I call Penny to me. I lock the back door, retreating once more to the butterfly room.

There are no Christmas cards this year, many friends and family having struck me off the list. The ones I have sit unopened in a pile. Clients have debated whether to give me one or not, some tactfully leaving it in sight of me, my taking it optional. I used to marvel about how popular my many adorning cards made me look, most of them from my clients, but that was before…

I had always reciprocated with Clive, one from each of us, but this year the house is in lockdown, secured from the merriment. I think about other people and other homes, likewise excluding themselves from the season. Christmas is an unavoidable anniversary. Other anniversaries are easier to block from the mindscape. For some the holiday can be about celebrating having got through the year, for others it is a time to look forward to the next. For many, it's a time to indulge their credit cards to the max, with a new year's resolution only of their being able to meet their debts. The capitalist Heaven on Earth.

I haven't always been so cynical, neither have I in the past been impervious to the excesses of this orgy of seasonal over-indulgence. But with the room devoid of garlands, I can sit and lick my wounds. Yet strangely, as I sit there I see the ghosts of Christmas past, every ornament on the tree recreated in my mind, heavily laden with memories of

Andrew. His card always had prominence of place on the mantelpiece and I would always have my annual bottle of Bailey's. With glass in hand we would sit and open our presents, my heart lifting while he enthused gratefully as the shiny wrapping revealed a new treasure.

We had a similar disposition and humour and we would pass glances between us reflecting our dry wit and sense of irony. I still have my annual bottle of Bailey's and glass in hand, but now it only serves to ease the lump in my throat.

My sister-in-law rings and enquires of my spirit. Anita is always considerate, as I reply "Fine" in the uniform way I always do, which even I find somewhat tedious. It is easier this way, as this is no doubt a pause between festivities at their house. I am sure Anita would appreciate the marked contrast, but I realise that even their turkey would have been somewhat poisoned this year, as they too had been very fond of Andrew.

Enough of this Bailey's. I stand up to go and make a coffee. With mug in hand I go upstairs to my bedroom, because there on the little green table amongst my books stands a little pot of undisturbed compost. The day before Christmas Eve a client had given me this little pot with hyacinth bulbs along with a bag of compost for potting. I remember her words as I look at them.

"These are for Andrew," she said.

As I grasp them to me, I realise at some deeper level that Andrew has responded once more to my Christmas wish. I never asked what motivated my client to give them to me, and she could have voiced one of many reasons. But God or spirit can work through a friend, and I also realise immediately that these precious bulbs will no doubt be in flower for Mothers' Day. I water it and whisper to it encouragingly as I stroke the little gold pot.

# 8

# *Thank You, Andrew*

*'If I can stop one heart from breaking, I shall not live in vain;*
*if I can ease one life from aching, or cool one pain,*
*or help one fainting robin unto his nest again,*
*I shall not live in vain.'*

—EMILY DICKINSON

So, that was Christmas – get over it. How often do you hear that phrase, "I'm thankful to have made it through"? Unusually, for the first time, there is none of the debris of the festive season to clear up. As for New Year resolutions, there are none other than my desire to get through the year.

I implore the ill-defined source, as I have come to view it, for guidance. I plead for it to show me what it is I am to do when the opportunity is presented. I consider that I shall know it when I feel the rising compulsion to follow my instincts. I ask my subconscious diviner to sift through possible avenues as they arise. Opportunities to meet people or venues to attend, I shall accept readily. Something deep within me convinces me that this is all I have to do at this moment. I am quite sure in the knowledge that at some point, by allowing this to happen, something will become apparent; I just have to remain confident.

I consider my contacts with Andrew. My confidence as far as that is concerned has taken a severe bashing, yet still I am drawn to attempt contact more regularly again. I feel he is still there in the background, still living away from home, having moved house. My desire to ring him is still unabated.

At the bottom of my bed is a small table underneath my bookshelves. Sitting upon its imitation green marble effect top is a photo of Andrew. I am stood next to him and we are laughing as we share some humorous interlude captured in time. Directly next to it is a flowering pot plant, the choice of which I change according to the seasons along with its bloom. Adjacent to this is the pot of hyacinths, which I watch keenly for signs of life. All of these are now being encroached upon by an ever-increasing quantity of books.

I'm still continually studying the frontiers of research into consciousness and its correlation to the wisdom of the ancients. The popular scientific paradigm is limited and does not follow the evidence. This in itself can be meaningless and purposeless and altogether reductionist. Deepak Chopra says it is something akin to taking a radio apart and wondering where the music goes, because they do not include consciousness. The early pioneers of quantum mechanics determined that the observed and the observer were not two different things. Traditional science said originally that the two are separate; but when you observe quantum effects it changes, they only becoming real when observed. The physicists said that, yes, it was true at micro scale; now the more contemporary ones say, yes, and at macro levels too.

Computer scientists realise how information is processed more like a hologram. In fact mathematicians, cosmologists, computer scientists and physicists are now converging, no longer able to exclude consciousness. They are led to believe that reality is somewhat expressed through holographic processing and that the universe is harmonically interconnected. A hologram is an image that contains the whole. If you take a beam of coherent light and split it into two, one part off an object and the other off a mirror, then combine the beams, the object can be recreated split into pieces. On first glance it reflects the whole, but every bit it is composed of contains the whole which it expresses. Buddha had taught that the universe was composed of jewels connected by golden threads of light. Current theories are based on the four per cent of reality that we see, but the rest is composed of dark matter and energy which science cannot yet grasp.

Andrew's once manager Will and his partner Carly came to visit this afternoon, carrying with them an addition to their family. Carly had been pregnant at the time; she had been disbelieving at first when I had called her on that day. She had been sure she had misheard; I expect she had hoped she had misheard. Andrew had been good friends with Carly, as he had with Will. Will had not been working that day and Andrew had been due to relieve Carly at 2 o'clock that afternoon. Numb with shock, she had soldiered on along with her colleague Chris, taking turns to address any queries from the hotel residents, giving brief respite to each of them as their tormented minds came to terms with the dawning reality of what had come to pass.

I had already spoken to the General Manager in my stupor, informing him that Andrew would not be at work today. He had spoken to both Carly and Chris, asking them to keep their counsel until the police had been in touch. On returning home, Carly informed Will of what had transpired and he had been thoroughly grief-stricken. Will had worked closely with Andrew, ever reliant on his fastidious tenacity. The respect and regard they had for each other was mutual, I had learned from my conversations with Andrew. It had been difficult for Will, Carly and the rest of the staff to struggle through the remainder of that year. The hotel had provided a counselling service. Token gesture that it was, Will in particular did not find it very adequate, having received only one session.

I was delighted to see these familiar faces. I had spoken to them rarely before and my primary purpose had always been to see Andrew. They had wanted to contact me, but because of staff confidentiality and the turmoil of the months that had passed they were reluctant to push the issue. I too had pondered how they had coped without their valued colleague and friend, prompting me to go through Andrew's 'phone logs for his regular contact numbers. I had called them directly. They were extremely pleased to hear from me, looking forward to their visit to share and discuss the depths to which they had plunged. They also needed to know answers to questions that had burned within the confines of their imagination this past eight months. These I would be able to satisfy, at the very least.

I had wondered if Carly was going to have a girl or a boy. She told me that on learning of Andrew's death she was sure it would be a boy. She did not know why she knew, as she had asked the hospital specifically not to disclose the gender of her baby. Now here he was, Euan, a brand new promise for this couple.

I told them how Clive and I had navigated the road through last year and answered the questions around Andrew's death with relative ease. What happened could not be undone, as neither could my profound belief in his continuing presence be. I dwelt little on the sadness, preferring instead to tell them of my contact and the insights and the knowledge I had gleaned, bypassing the metaphorical brick wall finality of death. Carly was enthused, to her it was only evidence of her own inclinations. Clive and I shared our recordings with them, leaving both of them quite amazed, Carly nodding, an acknowledgement of her deeper intuitions. Will, for the first time his world view distorting, accepted the truth of what he heard but was unsure how to respond.

Like many people, Will felt very uncomfortable dealing with death; I expect he felt very exposed. The problem for any sceptic is that to believe otherwise makes them feel a little out of control, possibly the victim of some inscrutable power. Strange, when you consider our very existence on Earth is beyond reason. The paranormal only adds additional twists and turns to, at its core, an otherwise uncentred, deconstructed and irrational world. Strange, that all the religions through the ages presenting a multitude of 'mind monsters' could ultimately be proved right by science itself. To award parapsychology any certification of reality or credibility would prompt our tenuous nervous systems to implode. What exactly would it do to our sensibilities if mankind in its infancy were told that yes, demons, fairies, angels, UFOs, aliens and entities do exist but you just can't see them? Many, or should I say most, people like things to be simplified. If you ask about the origins of life, people will invariably respond with 'the Big Bang'. It is not disputed. Yet if we contemplated the variety of possible ways the universe could have been physically formed or constituted, and within this very narrow range the possibilities conducive to life, it appears almost to be unimaginably improbable. Surely, I cannot be the only one who is not content with this conclusion?

Carly leaned forward and with lowered tones, addressing Clive and me, related a dream she had shortly after Andrew passed. She told us that she had dreamt it was late one night in the hotel. All the staff were present; she had it in mind that neither she nor the other staff could allow Andrew to leave. She knew that if he left then something bad would happen. It came to about midnight, by which time she was feeling a little more relaxed. Andrew seemed keen to go, assuring Carly that all was well and that nothing untoward would happen. Carly, now reassured by Andrew's overtures, no longer felt fearful as they bade each other good-bye and he departed, the time between 12.15 and 12.30 a.m. Carly now knew for the first time that the confirmed time of death as relayed by the police was between 12.00 and 2.00 a.m. in the morning.

The times of 12.00 - 12.30 seemed to have been a recurring theme in relation to people's experiences that had been brought to my attention. This only further reinforced what I had rapidly come to understand and take for granted. Carly, like all of us, had wrestled with the issues around Andrew's death. Was there something she could have done or said, or could she have changed the course of events? I believe that her vivid dream was probably facilitated by Andrew in some way. Like everyone who had been touched deeply, the message was always that he was ok and that, no, there was nothing that could have been done.

Will himself interjected at this stage with a dream that he had experienced. Andrew and he were walking up a dark tunnel. Will could barely keep up with him so he called for him to slow down. He could feel the ring on Andrew's finger glancing against his own hand. Andrew had laughed, as Will realised that he would not catch up with him and had to remain behind and carry on. Although Will had discounted this as 'no more than a dream', he had felt shaken when he awoke.

There was a shared warmth between us and I hoped, as we parted, that this nice young couple could continue with the fonder memories of Andrew, having laid some of their nightmare to rest and additionally had sparked the light of the possibility of Andrew's continued presence. We would meet again.

• • •

I still by and large lived life in the present, one day at a time. I saw my counsellor once a month, sharing with her my more intimate thoughts and of course my latest contact with Andrew. At one point, listening together to the voice of 'Chokas' replaying on my 'phone, Simone was as intrigued as me. Reflecting my own reservations, she cautioned me. This is an ongoing dilemma for me. Between visits, I had cut down considerably on my attempts, ever cautious of a repeat performance. I held the mobile away from my ear – any further hint of that presence would have resulted in my throwing it across the room.

It crossed my mind that Andrew may have moved on, as his responses were not as strong as they had been. Neither were they as immediate. However, I was now able to sleep with the light off again. The promise of a good night's sleep was mine once more.

Mothers' Day approached, it was everywhere I looked. It was in the shops, flowers, cards - the celebration of motherhood. Like Christmas, I chose to ignore it, I chose to overlook the snippets of conversations I heard of family get-togethers. I blanked the adorning flowers and cards I saw in my clients' houses.

The day arrived. It was a Sunday, the day I used to see Andrew. This time last year, I too had received a beautiful card and a bouquet of flowers. At twelve midday, I would normally ring Andrew with our approximate time of arrival. I decided I should call him anyway!

I felt less stupid doing it by the fact that Clive had gone to visit his father in a residential old people's home. I sat within the stillness of the bedroom, deciding merely to press the record button and sit quietly. Wherever he was, I was sure that if he could pick up on anything this would be the day. There was a possibility he would be able to communicate. I looked long and hard at the photograph of Andrew perched on the shelf at the bottom of the bed. I exhaled heavily, in a way common to the sadness of defeat. I picked up the 'phone and tentatively pressed the playback.

There was a chance and Andrew had taken it. In a swell of emotion I clasped my head; I thought I might pass out in the giddy excitement of the moment. Andrew had truly excelled himself this time. There was a kind of breakthrough noise, like a rap, followed by two distinct tunes rather like some clever individual with a pencil. This was punctuated at the end by the name "An-dr-eew"! This more than made up for any difficulty I had experienced with 'Chokas'.

Almost triumphantly, I handed Clive the `phone as he entered the house. "Yes," he said as he handed it back to me, "it definitely says 'Andrew'." Proving anything to anybody was of no concern to me, this was an opportunity for my soul. They say you can always delude other people, but you cannot delude yourself. I knew from that moment without a shadow of a doubt, if there had been any doubt, that it was just yes, yes, yes. I think I could have lit a gas fire from about twenty feet with the pure energy that sparked from within. I put the `phone down.

My sister-in-law had invited us over for a get-together that week-end. I think this year had changed all of us in some way. Conversation was kinder all round, priorities further honed. I looked forward to going; Birmingham, here we come.

It was a bright, warm late spring day, an enticing buffet laid before us to go with my coffee. Penny ran herself ragged round the garden with my other brother's dog Mitzi. It was nice, mixing with the varying ages of my younger brother's daughters. The day flowed lightly with much laughter, interjected with memories of Andrew. My sister-in-law Anita took me aside. "I have a message for you," she told me, her eyes holding mine as we sat ourselves together.

Anita told me she had been to see a medium. The visit had been prompted one evening when she had been out with a friend to a local restaurant. A lady had approached them, excusing herself as she passed them a card. Sitting down to the meal, Anita examined the card; it was from a spiritual medium. Her curiosity aroused, Anita had felt compelled to make an appointment. I remembered vaguely a few weeks ago Anita mentioning having been handed a card in the restaurant. However, now she told me that she had booked to see this lady. I think she had been additionally compelled by her daughter having recently received a diagnosis of thyroid cancer.

During the course of the reading, Anita had become increasingly impressed by the seemingly accurate facts that this lady conveyed to her. It was during the course of the reading, Anita told me, that a young man had interjected. A few pertinent facts were touched on around the circumstances of Andrews's demise. The medium further disclosed that there was a teddy bear with a bell and that she could see Andrew looking at it and putting it down. Immediately, I rummaged through my mental filing cabinet. Andrew had often bought me fluffy mementos during the course of his life. But I was sure that none of them had a bell, particularly in these days of health and safety.

Having disclosed all that she could remember, Anita kissed me on the forehead, telling me it was from Andrew. Excited, no, but intrigued, yes, a lot of what she said rested on my finding a bear with a bell. On returning home that evening, I shook each and every one of my furry companions, but no, not one with a bell. I rang Andrew's dad's wife, since she too had an impressive collection of fluffy friends, but no, not one with a bell.

Then the very next day she rang me to say yes, they had a teddy bear with a bell. It had been Andrew's dad's bear that he'd had as a child, kept in the attic. Andrew would have been aware of this bear as he was frequently in the attic removing and storing various items for his dad and Sheila. The case appeared to be solved. The only problem was, like the whole entirely subjective area of paranormal phenomena, I too found myself questioning the validity of someone else's experience. I could not doubt what I had encountered but still found myself questioning my sister-in-law's version. My critical, analytical mind went into overdrive. Did she lead or was she led? If I was not there, how could I know? Oh, bugger!

This threw me into something of a quandary, questioning the very nature of this book. I could no more deny her her own belief any more than she could deny me mine. So I made my mind up that I would see this medium. Birmingham, here I come again! I booked it for one evening after I had finished work, driving all the way to Birmingham with both Clive and Penny in tow. With almost a hint of disquieting arrogance, I deemed that if she could not pick up on my loss, then a medium she was not...

• • •

We arrive at a fairly modern, newly built housing estate, finding the house with five minutes to go. I knock on the door, filled with the anticipation of what I might learn. The door is opened by a young man, indicating a door to the right. The medium is busy with someone else in an adjacent room. I seat myself on a comfortable, blue two-seater sofa opposite a forty-two inch LCD television. She is running 10... 20... 30... 40 minutes late. As her previous appointment leaves, a petite younger middle-aged woman with long, blonde curly hair smiles at me. I am told that my name has been perpetually on her mind all that day.

"Hmmph!" I respond, as I seat myself at the small wooden kitchen table. Sitting there with her hands over her eyes, she attempts to make contact with the realm beyond.

It would appear that everybody else's relatives were available that evening except mine. Exasperated, she asks me who it is I want to contact. Having already written off the paper tokens in my pocket amounting to thirty-five pounds, I concede that it is my son who has prompted my visit. No, it was not a car crash, illness etcetera, and so on until she has exhausted her list of possibilities. Suddenly looking inspired, she asks me if he was in the forces. "Yes," I affirm. She sees him now, in army uniform complete with brass buckle. She watches closely for my reaction. Was he a policeman? A sailor? Bingo, I think, well done, it only took twenty attempts. She tells me she has trouble distinguishing between uniforms. I agree that it can be confusing, as I often get sailors mixed up with soldiers. She then asks me if he drowned.

This woman is in difficulty and so I decide to terminate the reading; much as I enjoy comedy, this is not the time. I consider docking some of her fee towards the petrol.

Despondent, I join Clive in the car. He has assumed from the time that has elapsed that the reading has been going well. I am so thankful that I have not relied on this woman entirely for my salvation, because disappointment would have been an understatement. I take it that it must have been a bad hair day.

We call on my sister-in-law en route home. Clive warns me not to be too brutal in my judgement of the medium, for Anita's sake. Anita opens the door, expecting me. "Well?" she asks. That is enough.

"Rubbish," I respond. Clive glares at me sideways. However, I continue, perhaps she was not up to performing as she normally would. Anita is disappointed and a little perplexed as she had been totally convinced by her reading. I assure her that it in no way impacts on me personally, and it didn't. Having said that, it might have had I not been already entirely confident of Andrew's existence. For now, a mug of coffee more than meets my most pressing needs, and can I have another before I go?

Our journey home passes humorously as I recount to Clive word for word what must have been considered even by the medium herself a totally disastrous reading. Still, it has scratched an itch. The mobile 'phone is a far cheaper proposition and does not detract from my minute allowance in any way.

• • •

It's Andrew's birthday today. Last year at this time Andrew had a motorbike from us; it had sat in the garage awaiting a suitable time for delivery. He had been as excited as a five year old with a new toy, a pleasure I had shared. He inspected every inch of it, checking levers and switches and stroking its bodywork. I had never wanted him to have a motorbike, but the prospect of buying a car and its resultant running costs was beyond his means presently. I figured that at the age of twenty-eight he was sufficiently responsible, alleviating any reservations I had. He would be able to visit his friends more frequently.

I remember that day, arriving in Buxton, and the temporary relief at seeing his bike benignly parked and secured.

I can still see his now boxed helmet through the garage window, barely used. My attempts tonight to share these memories of the bike with Andrew go unrewarded. I get no acknowledgement of the day. I grow frustrated as I try several times. I am curious as to why he will not respond on this day above all others. It had never been this difficult. I wonder, did this signal the end of our contact? Did it mean that the extension of favour from the spiritual realm had come to an end? I thought it might come to this eventually, but I had thought in a strange kind of way that Andrew, always having been creative, had secured some kind of loophole.

I castigate myself inwardly, realising how silly my thinking has become. I further ponder that, thoroughly convinced as I was of Andrew's continuing presence, it was perhaps deemed by 'the upper echelons' that I no longer required the intensive care of visitation that I had so desperately needed in the beginning. All these things and more, I mull over. I further wonder if this omission is more by way of a statement. If spirit by its very nature is in receipt of the bigger picture, then maybe 'a birthday' is of no consequence, given the expanse of infinity of all that is. I shall try again, when I recover from this disappointment.

• • •

It's not uncommon for me to awake once or twice a night. Hot flushes, which I affectionately call power surges, cause me to reach out for my ever-present bottle of water. However, on this one occasion, reaching out for my customary drink, my eyes are drawn naturally to the bottom of the bed as I bring the bottle to my lips. Stopping mid-movement, I freeze as I see a translucent Andrew looking at me. Unmoving, my eyes flick to the right and left of this apparition. I note the familiar gap of light from my blacked-out curtains, allowing just a sliver of moonlight. Repeatedly I blink and narrow my eyes, trying to ascertain if I am seeing what I think I am seeing. I am not frightened in any way; I honestly cannot say I am startled, just a little mesmerised.

I take in his form, his right arm raised with his thumb and forefinger forming a circle in front of his right eye, at first reminiscent of a dart thrower's stance. I struggle to understand the significance of this. The image remains unmoved, as we apparently just look at each other like a frozen frame in time. Still, once more I look to the right and the left, to determine any trick of light or imagination. All calm, all peaceful, all natural, a melding of spirits. His appearance now dissipates into specks of light, rather like a residual transporter image in Star Trek. My arm now re-animates into finishing the task of satisfying my thirst.

Having done so, I go to the bathroom. Standing within the dim moonlit room, I attempt to recapture the image of Andrews's stance in front of the mirror. I raise my right hand to my right eye, emulating the posture of a dart thrower. I think, "Why like that?" Andrew never threw darts. I think through other connotations and suddenly realise that it could quite easily have been an 'ok' sign, or even an indication of his 'keeping an eye' on me. Yes, I am completely convinced it was either one of these, laying to rest the assumption of dart throwing.

Pulling the covers back over me, I smile as I turn over. I am neither excited nor perturbed, strangely. It is the one thing I have not expected. I contemplate the prospect of having a higher self, the self that knows far and above our waking consciousness, transcending the reality we all build for ourselves. I believe that it is because of this closer working relationship we have shared over the last year, it more readily engages with me. It has assisted in our communication through the thin divide that separates us, wordlessly.

It is almost like this life is a gap between reunions. It is at times like this I can grasp it, understanding it to be perfectly normal and not at all disturbing.

I tell Clive about my having seen Andrew. I do not dwell on it for too long with Clive, because strangely in the cold light of day I am very conscious - or should I say sensitive - about any hint of disbelief. It is not because I do not doubt for one minute that Clive will believe me, but hearing myself say it feels as uncomfortable as if I am hearing it from someone else. So there I leave it. I make my mind up that I am unlikely to repeat it to anyone – it just happened. I expect that if it had been the only thing that happened, I will be talking about it daily like a born-again Christian; but because it is not, I really don't feel inclined...

• • •

There are times when it is about reflection and, as it draws near to the eve of Andrew's death, I sit and sift through the book of condolences handed to me at the funeral. Some entries, among many others, exemplify the void left by Andrew for his many friends and colleagues. The following is a letter from Andrew's manager, Will:

*'You're my best at that!' How many times have you heard me say that mate? Lots... That's because you were!*

*How are you doing Andrew? Hope you're ok and in a happy place, with lots of paint! Miss you loads, my friend, and I feel different without you! I keep wishing you would walk in through the door at work and start the shift off with one of your crazy anecdotes, cheer me up and get me in the mood for a busy day!*

*You were a top class, irreplaceable employee and I admired your care and attention of people and also your determination to get a job done. I would of employed ten of you if I could, but alas you were a one and only! The hotel will never be the same without you.*

*I don't recall a single moment of time spent in your company which I didn't enjoy! You were awesome to be around and a fantastic, passionate and sensitive person and I wish you could see how much you are missed! It was an honour to know you and I'll never forget you!*

*Will xx*

And this one from a colleague who worked closely with Andrew:

*Hey there Andy, how's it going?*

*There is something I have been meaning to tell you... You're ace. REALLY ace. You've been a fantastic rod of support at the hotel, teaching me lots I didn't already know about the job and always going out of your way to help when I got myself into one of my ridiculous (and usually completely avoidable) work related situations. Also, you've always coped with my cry-baby over-reactions to these situations admirably! More than that though, you've been a great friend. I can't recall a single moment in your company that I haven't been happy to have known you.*

*In short, you mean the world to me and I can tell you by speaking to a lot of those that worked with you that they felt the same way. I'm taking this opportunity to say thank you for everything... It just breaks my heart that I never took the time to tell you this in person.*

*Rest in peace my friend, I'll never forget you.*

*Chris xxx*

Tonight, this evening last year, Andrew left us. I attempt to try and contact him. Yes, Andrew does respond. Bittersweet and curious that he acknowledges this event and not his birthday. I am sad as I replay his tune...

# 9

## Believe Me

*'In order to realise your destiny, you must be willing
to release your history.'*

—KARL SCHMIDT

I have covered the most emotionally turbulent period of my life. If this
had been a purely physical challenge, its equivalent would have been
climbing the north face of the Eiger - and coming down again can be
just as tricky. Endurance tests don't come much harder!

One of the main difficulties I have encountered is the terrain I have
had to cover. I have never had problems with my credibility before, but
inevitably this does come with the territory. People, I find, do tend to
go out of their way to distract me from my insistence that Andrew has
made contact. This is compounded by the discomfort of any interaction
with a bereaved mother customarily being a 'no-go' area. This marginal-
ises me somewhat, discouraging me from promoting any conversation
in relation to anything remotely Andrew-orientated. Yet before the
event, Andrew had been such a large part of my conversational input,
naturally. It would appear that I have been demoted in his absence.

I don't know quite how my brothers perceive it all. I sometimes
think that perhaps they see it as a stage that I was likely to go through.
They have been very supportive, each in their own way, life permitting.

I wished on occasion that I felt as though they took me seriously. If they did, then I apologise; but conversely, if this was more as a consequence of their own discomfort, I understand. It is very difficult when, out of the blue, there is a direct challenging of world views.

My counsellor was quite convinced that I had contact with Andrew. I would allow her to hear my more interesting ones. If she believed nothing, then certainly the 'Chockas' episode had driven home the hidden reality of another dimension. Simone imparted to me that her daughter had studied parapsychology at university when younger and asked if I wanted her to make enquiries of her ex-colleagues. It was undeniable that what I had achieved in my tenacity to make contact was extremely unusual and perhaps unique. I knew that Simone believed me, which was very important to me. People had never questioned either my integrity or honesty before. This contrasted remarkably with how the world perceived me now. This was the most frustrating thing, although I daresay it would provoke a similar response in me should someone inform me of their daily forays down to the bottom of the garden to feed an invisible gnome! I understood this.

But when you know for absolute sure that you haven't stage managed something or deluded yourself in any way? No-one could have been more critical or even sceptical on occasion, but still I could not avoid the curiously obvious evidence I had encountered on so regular a basis. It was never that I had just not faced up to the facts; the facts had been blatantly clear from the outset. Sometimes people are haunted by a deep intuition which they struggle to contain with their more rational nature, but then quite often wish they had listened to this inner prompting. In the beginning, I struggled daily, analysing where this overwhelming conviction that Andrew was there came from, in light of everything I knew. This in itself isolates one from society's norms and, yes, I said I would like Simone to ask her daughter if she had any colleagues I could discuss it with.

The church, although polite, had largely frowned upon me, and yet I had done far better than many regular churchgoers. I had remained healthy and my mental faculties had maintained their clarity, by and large. Their list of bereavement criteria had somewhat passed me by. Had it not been for my technology, I would have written off all my sentient feelings, as gradually they were alleviated and may well have been left behind in the mists of time. How many people have said to me in the past that they had felt their mother around today, or said "I felt he was with me" but had not been able to capture it. I have been able both to capture it and replay it.

I suppose half of me wants to say to the parapsychologists, "There you are, it's true." Another part of me wants to address those with spiritual inclination, "There you are, it's true." But most of all I want to extend my experiences to those who have lost people, mother, fathers, children or friends. I want to say with absolute confidence, "There you are, it's true."

• • •

The next time I saw Simone, she told me that her daughter had made enquiries. Unfortunately, Liverpool University was not currently studying that particular aspect of paranormal activity. They had passed my name on to a particular parapsychologist who was studying this area. Aware as I was that the whole subject was in 'the land of if', most of our exchanges were by email. This is not my first chosen method of communication. I prefer the swift exchange of audible interaction, picking up on nuances, inferences and innuendos, all in all a far more satisfactory experience. However, this did not deter me from getting my evidence at least somewhere for an educated view.

The following passages are brief excerpts from my diary submitted to the professional parapsychologist, to serve as a summary of the most important events in this narrative. The case is still ongoing.

• • •

I thank you for making contact. It has been quite a journey for me, but without doubt whatever the outcome of your interest/investigation, it has left me with quiet, unquestionable belief in something more fantastical to life than our own senses can perceive.

I am aware that it is in large part down to my own perception, learning, belief system, personal philosophy etc; but what I will unfold to you is backed quite substantially with a good deal of evidence and testimony raising to my mind (not just mine) an incredible occurrence…

I had been led to believe that a sense of the departed presence is a common feeling among the recently bereaved and I wanted anything I felt recorded. However, I had not envisaged the experience to be ongoing, manifesting in a variety of ways… It came over regularly, consistently and at times without any real intention/expectation by me and indeed (quite importantly!) over a long period of time (to date).

### 22nd June, 2011

That evening I spoke to Andrew after he had finished work… [and there] was no indication that anything was wrong at this time.

That night I awoke as a vivid picture of Andrew abruptly entered a dream I was having; it was a picture only of his face lying down with his eyes shut. This was immediately followed by what I thought was my ‘phone ringing. I scrabbled for my mobile, slightly panicked by my vision and dark thoughts. I was relieved to find it had not registered an incoming call and obviously at the time I assumed ‘nightmare’ and promptly went to sleep.

### 23rd June, 2011

I rang Andrew as usual at about 12 p.m. but received no reply. I repeatedly called but with no response I decided to leave a message… [then later] decided to embark for Buxton…

When I arrived, his curtains were drawn on his 2nd floor flat but a light on in his spare room. I knew then that something bad had happened as the vision of the night before replayed in my mind…

On entry, myself and two officers walked down the hall, I saw a scarf trapped over the door whereupon I pointed and announced that he had hung himself. The door was opened and Andrew fell heavily to the floor.

### 24th June, 2011

I was standing in the back garden when I thought I heard my ‘phone go. I searched through my pockets, realising it was indoors. I went inside commenting to Clive that I thought I’d heard my ‘phone. He responded that it had not which I already suspected. However, I felt compelled to take a time check – 12.40 p.m. I then went through my call log of the day before and it correlated exactly with the time I had left my request for an 'ok' call from Andrew. This I found quite heartening as Andrew never missed his returning calls!

### 25th June, 2011

Andrew was to be best man at his friend's (John) wedding. He rang me having tracked down my number. During the course of the call he was very keen to learn if Andrew had left any letters. He then went on excitedly about an extraordinary dream in which he had received a letter. On opening and reading the contents, he dropped it in shock – the letter said, 'By the time you read this I shall be gone, I'm so sorry, please find a cheque attached for the cost of the suit'. He then awoke quite distressed…

On the run up to the funeral, I longed to hold [Andrew]. I had one of two vivid dreams just before his committal. I dreamt he came to the top of the driveway as I was outside – he appeared to be a boy of about thirteen or so dressed in familiar attire of that age. I threw my arms around him and beckoned him inside which he declined. The dream over, I awoke feeling I had really felt him. We had not been resident in this house when Andrew was that age.

### 26th June, 2011

Clive and I were walking the dog in the country when suddenly she froze looking ahead and upwards on the path. We also stopped to see what was spooking her, there was nothing we could see or perceive. However, both Clive and I had the strangest feeling that Andrew had come to see the dog as he had intended that weekend.

### 5th July, 2011

The entire time since the morning of Andrew's passing I prayed he remained with me subliminally supporting me. I was strangely peaceful… During the committal, Andrew's flagged coffin (ex-Navy) would not lower. After repeated attempts, we decided that people be given leave. After I approached the coffin and kissed the rose, the coffin began to lower, startling me…

**6th July, 2011**

Sheila rang – when Andrew's father took out Andrew's watch on return from the funeral, it was stopped at 12.15.

**8th July, 2011**

The police inform me that Andrew took his life between 12 and 2 a.m. on the morning of the 23rd.

**11th July, 2011**

I have a very strong desire to continually play the very personal pieces of the music I chose for the funeral in the car as I return to work today. But, rather than invoke wretchedness, it brings the peace and calm of the day…

**13th July, 2011**

The undertaker Neil called to arrange collection of the ashes. Without prompt, he tells us how extremely unusual that Andrew's coffin had not lowered. He'd spoken to the crem staff and they had suggested it may have been the flag covering the sensors. Tom was adamant that he was very used to draping and ensuring that the sensors were clear.

**23rd July, 2011**

Eureka, contact made with Andrew. I had bought a dowsing pendulum with some expectation. This night, I tried. I just felt warmth as I attempted to dowse, but the intent together with any influence I had on the pendulum made me frustrated. I would not be satisfied if I myself had produced the outcome.

I felt confident that tonight was different. I had flirted with the 'phone to a tune of fourteen attempts via the recorder. However, although I felt he had responded on two occasions in the past few days (retained), I could not be sure.

Before I activated the 'phone recorder, I asked Andrew to tap twice if he was there:

*"Sweetheart, are you there?"*
TAP-TAP

Assuming that Andrew was responding, I said,
*"Andrew, is that you?"*
TAP-TAP
I decided at this point that it would be better to suggest,
*"Tap once for 'yes'."*
TAP
*"And tap twice for 'no', then maybe we can communicate."*
TAP-TAP
*"Are you around, Andrew?"*
TAP-TAP, followed by a distinct and loud single TAP then another TAP.
*"Are you surrounded by love and light?"*
TAP, but then followed by TAP-TAP
*"Are you with my dad?"*
TAP
*"Or with your dad's dad?"*
TAP-TAP and then another TAP-TAP
*"Is this world combined with ours?"*
TAP, then TAP-TAP followed by TAP
*"Can you go wherever you want?"*
TAP
*"Do you like the dog?"*
TAP
*"Do you know what I mean about the dog?"*
TAP
*"Do you hear the music?"* (I meant the funeral music I played in the car.)
There was no answer.
*"Do you like the music?"*
TAP
*"Goodnight sweetheart."*

When I played it back, I heard the first responses and bounded out of bed to my partner Clive. "Andrew's alive, he's here, I have made contact." Winning the lottery pales in comparison to how I felt. We both listened – the crackling static of energy approaching and receding with every response was electrifying.

Considering the circumstances under which Andrew had passed, I felt the urgent way in which he responded reflected my son torn between sadness, regret and otherwise but that in some strange way he had leave to support me.

### 24th July, 2011

Andrew's father's new wife known to Andrew some seventeen years (a good relationship) told me she had dreamed (vividly) that she had been in the bedroom and come across a book which she placed on her lap. She became conscious of Andrew nearby laughing, she remonstrated with him for this only for him to indicate to the book she had placed her hand over. As she lifted her hand she saw 'Andrew Thomas Parton' to which he said, "Well Sheila, you always said you could read me like a book, so there it is." At this point, she awoke. Sheila also said that her otherwise reliable clock in the flat had stopped at just gone 12.15 a.m. However, she could not be sure of the day.

### 25th July, 2011

Received a second recording (loud responses) from Andrew but unfortunately I can't hear my voice/questions…

### July/August

Continually trying to make contact with Andrew. I try mainly last thing at night. Sometimes during the day. Occasionally I get weak replies.

There is a difficulty in communication; I have suggested 1x tap for yes, 2x taps for no and 3x taps to send love. Through these I have received acknowledgements and his sending his love. Questions answered are harder to obtain.

Brilliant! Asked Andrew if he could say a word, hum a tune or whistle – got him whistling directly after the word whistle. Still amazed – getting acknowledgements and sending love.

Getting a very distinct energy noise. I have grown familiar with this as it was there when I originally contacted Andrew. It is indicating to me that spirit/soul energy is present but not communicating.

This noise, although it can be described as static or in similar descriptive terms, is a fairly unique noise and not easily defined. However, I do have recordings of it.

### August 2nd, 2011

Awoken by 3x taps to my door followed by "Are you alright, Jacquie?" Well-spoken male, assumed at first it was my partner. All quiet, don't really know about this one other than I was sure it happened.

### August 5th, 2011

I asked that if Andrew was finding it difficult to communicate, maybe I could visit him – had a very vivid dream.

I dreamt I was going on exercise in the back of an army lorry (ex-army), it was very dark with no light or window. The driver asked me to disembark and go for a coffee (I thought that this was most peculiar). As I wandered off I was more concerned with how I would get back. Found myself in a town – went into a carpet shop to look at rugs. I told the male assistant I didn't want an expensive one as it was for my son's bedroom and that he had died and it would not get much wear. He was very empathetic. I left the shop and wandered on and saw a middle-aged lady with glasses on in front of a whiteboard under a canvass gazebo in front of a two-seater leather settee and two chairs. She told me, "Andrew will be with you in a moment", but then as she closed to me she smiled and added, "His face was soaking wet when we found him!" This was strange as I have never heard that said before.

Andrew came from behind, made to touch my arm immediately saying "I'm sorry, I'm so sorry, Mum." He was wearing a grey/white suit, his hair was slightly longer (no beard), his skin was pale with a grey line running down his throat under his chin which he stroked remarking that he hadn't got long because as I could see (he did say see), his voice was weak. I stood up and said "It's ok sweetheart", moving towards him incredulously I just said "So, can you see me anytime?" to which he replied "Yes I can, but I don't." I said, "So, those books I've read, are they true?" He responded, "Yes." I felt time was running out as the background started to fade to dark, so hastily I said, "So, what do you do here?"

Andrew answered that 'there was a lot to do, lots to do'; I asked that if he, say, wanted to learn the guitar he just had to think of it, to which he looked at me as if to say – as if? But then he replied, "Pretty much." At this point it went dark and I woke up.

## 27th August, 2011

Went to `phone my brother Tim to find Andrew's number displayed.

## 2nd October, 2011

After starting to write this log I picked up my `phone to see if Andrew was around to find his number displayed.

This morning I had asked Andrew if he could access the `phone while it sat and it had appeared to be accessed in the closed position because his name was displayed.

During this day, I was telling Clive about this curiosity and he suggested asking Andrew for a text, to which I laughingly responded that I had asked him to play with his `phone already.

## 3rd October, 2011

I returned home from work. Clive said he had received an email from Andrew. Apparently, he had received an automated 'Friend acceptance' from Andrew's Facebook. He can't explain how that could happen. We cannot access Andrew's Facebook account which is why it is still there.

## 7th October, 2011

Visited Andrew's dad and his wife Sheila in Buxton to deliver one of Andrew's paintings they wanted.

I let Sheila and his dad listen to my recordings i.e. tappings and whistle. Tried to get Andrew to respond (negative). The home `phone rang twice while I was there. As I was leaving Sheila called to me and handed me the `phone. She had checked it as I rose to leave in case it was important; the number displayed was their own number. Sheila rang BT that day to see if a fault could cause this to happen but BT told her it couldn't happen and that they could not explain it.

That evening I thanked Andrew for his support, he tapped three times on opening the recording.

## 12th October, 2011

Two weeks ago – asked Andrew if he could come up with a teddy or some flowers for my birthday. Today, a client on my departure went into the lounge – took her flowers out of her vase and put them in a carrier bag. On querying this, she said that she felt she wanted to give me them.

## 19th October, 2011

Thought I had contact with Andrew – tried new recording and got the strangest electronic charge tapping – I believe his energy was near. Made me tingle all down my side, slightly uncomfortable.

## November, 2011

Getting fewer contacts now. Strange electronic energy noise – like energy drawing closer…

During the course of this November day, I decided to go through all my recordings during the day. I wrote the numbered recordings in the back of my work diary cross referencing them with remarks as to what was on them. I deleted the ones of little interest i.e. poor. The intention that evening was to download them to the computer, primarily for posterity (in case I lost my `phone). But also to hear them as I did from time to time on the amplified speakers.

## 8 p.m.

Clive and I downloaded to computer and listened to some on the amplified speakers. One recording which had nothing on other than a very loud electrical presence had been superimposed between lunchtime and that evening. It started with a very loud rap… like a breakthrough noise, then deadly silence, then: "Chockas (my spelling) wait in the night." Clear as a bell and very measured with little intonation. Clive looked at me and said "What the hell was that?" I was

TAP ONCE FOR YES

shocked, mainly because that recording was some 2 weeks old and had not been there (if it had I would have desisted long before today). Clive continued, "Because it sure as hell is not Andrew!" I immediately checked my `phone. It was on! This was too much; I deleted everything off my `phone. Clive downloaded everything to disk which is where it is to this day.

Clive remonstrated with me about going round like an ice cream wagon attracting goodness knows what. I felt dreadful and very frightened. I had not considered the implications of what I had been doing

Clive and I searched various spellings of this 'Chockas'. The only one we found was with regards to the Torah. As we scanned, our eyes were drawn immediately to 'defilement'. I really don't know? We had to sleep with the lights on...

Quite apart from my diary entries, this for me proved categorically beyond a shadow of doubt that, if nothing else, it evidenced a dimension other than what we are aware of.

No-one had access to that `phone except me (carried continually as we have no landline). That particular `phone could not duplicate recordings over the same allocated number (once deleted, that number was gone). Therefore, that voice transposed onto an original recording between lunch and evening. The remarks I made against that number were – 'strong electrical presence'. The original was made some 2x weeks earlier...

I can honestly say I felt it was a warning to let it go.

**November, 2011**

During this time, I invited the local pastor Maria to visit me. I cannot believe I had to admit to what I had been exploring and the outcome in order for her to bless the house (any port in a storm!). Of course, this was swiftly followed by the vicar calling on me and abruptly reminding me of the powers of darkness (felt pretty humble at the time).

**20th December, 2011**

Asked Andrew if he could give me some flowers for Christmas. Customer gave me a pot of hyacinths – she just said, "These are for Andrew." I expect them to flower for Mothers' Day.

I started tentatively to try and contact Andrew again. I remember holding the `phone away from my ear on playback in case 'Chockas' responded to which if it was the case I would probably throw the `phone. However, to date I do not think he has…

I cannot say I got much if anything (possibly vague) over the Christmas period. This was a little disappointing…

## January/February, 2012

Using my work `phone now. Still getting the odd contact with Andrew, again some better than others. Had some strange ones – weird noises and erratic tapping.

## 5th March, 2012

Andrews's manager Will visited with his partner Carly who also worked with Andrew.

Carly told me of a dream she had: the whole of the staff at the hotel where Andrew worked stayed behind one evening to ensure Andrew did not go home in case he did not return. It got to about after twelve when Andrew told Carly he was just nipping home and that he would be ok. Carly attempted to stop him as she was concerned but Andrew insisted he would be alright. She was satisfied that he seemed happy and off he went. The time was she said about 12.00 - 12.30.

Will commented, after I had discussed my experiences with him, that he had that peculiar thing with his `phone where Andrew's number kept displaying. He also dreamed that he was following Andrew down a dark passage. He could not see him very clearly but knew he was there as Andrew's ring on his finger kept glancing against his own hand as he struggled to keep up. He called to Andrew to slow down as he could not go so fast.

This again tied in with earlier entries. Again, it appears that Carly – through Andrew – had what she considered one of her fears answered. That being, that if she had known, could any action she had taken have averted what happened. It is now my considered belief (in light of contact people feel they have had) that the answers given are not necessarily ones you think you want or desire, but only the affirmation, whatever form it takes, that is deemed necessary by spirit.

**18th March, 2012**

Fantastic! Contacted Andrew at midday. Three loud bangs followed by a very distinct tune ending with "AN-DR-EW"! Really clear. Over the moon, absolutely wonderful. What a fantastic Mothers' Day present. Earlier I had been pleased that my hyacinths had flowered over this weekend!

I had this drumming on earlier recordings, but this recording came over as a well-orchestrated combination. Now I knew that it was a new twist from what I believe to be coming from Andrew. The tunes are all different, so now when I hear them I have the feeling that he knows that I know it is him, no need for questions or answers.

**March, 2012**

My sister-in-law Anita who resides in Birmingham told me that she went out for a meal with a friend. On finding their seats, a lady came over and handed her a card outlining medium and spiritual services. Anita queried why she had been handed this, the lady responded that she was out with her sister who was a medium and that she had asked her to hand my sister-in-law a card.

The reading was extremely pertinent both in relation to Anita's family and also to Andrew. She did however conclude by talking of a teddy bear with a bell.

When she related this story, I immediately turned over my bedroom for a teddy with a bell. Having exhausted my soft toys I rang Sheila who in her turn looked for a teddy with a bell. The next day Sheila rang telling me that she had turned to Alex (Andrew's dad) if he knew of any teddy she had with a bell. Surprisingly, Alex said that he had a bear from his being a child in the attic in a box with a bell in its ear. Apparently, Andrew went in the loft frequently for both his dad and Sheila with them both being disabled.

At first I thought this was amazing, and obviously this medium was worth seeing. However, I made an appointment one evening, driving all the way to Birmingham with some expectation. The result was extremely disappointing!

So the upshot is that I am not sure, although I do not doubt Anita... The details about Andrew were quite accurate and on first sight only verified by me (omitted as they are quite personal).

**27<sup>th</sup> April, 2012**

Had to go to the dentist, always super nervous about this. Went to McDonald's drive-thru for a coffee before going. Contacted Andrew - responded. The only thing is, it spooked me a bit as I don't really get good responses during the day so when I parked up at the dentist's I tried again and just said, "Andrew, are you always there?" - a loud bang.

**3<sup>rd</sup> May, 2012**

Andrew's birthday. Tried really hard to contact for about the last three days. Nothing.

**30<sup>th</sup> May, 2012**

The following caused me some problem and debate as to whether or not to include it in my statements. The main area of difficulty is that I thought it may undermine my credibility if what I have written does not already strain credulity. However, I will, as to not do so would feel uncomfortably dishonest on my part. I leave it to you.

I have been experiencing the onset of hot flushes for some two years. Obviously, this awakens me a couple of times a night to ingest water before turning over once more. This one night, I awoke and saw a translucent Andrew at the bottom of the bed. It did not alarm me in the slightest. What did puzzle me as I stared was that he appeared to be emulating the stance of a darts thrower. His fingers and thumb forming a circle fronting his right eye. The image faded. I went to the bathroom, and in the dim light, I mirrored this position asking myself, "Why like that?" I concluded that it was probably nothing to do with darts (which he never played) but quite probably an 'ok' or a 'keeping an eye' on me. I was pretty convinced at the time.

**22<sup>nd</sup> June, 2012**

The eve of Andrew's death [anniversary] – received contact – another distinct tune. When I heard it, I `phoned back so to speak and thanked him and asked him if he was there if I needed him and he responded 'yes'!

I have reached the conclusion that spirit (or whatever term you choose to use) does not necessarily answer questions you feel you need answers to, so much as conveys what they feel you should know or understand. For example, Andrew appears to have satisfied very deep and profound concerns of everyone who believes they have experienced something. As for me, I have felt encompassed by his presence and love which is reflected in my many recorded contacts…

After the devastation of last year's event, I have arrived at a new awareness/consciousness. Most people struggle to find a spiritual element to their lives. This year has left me with a sense of knowing, yet not knowing quite what it is…

A scientist once said, "It's good to be open minded, but not so open that your brains fall out".

• • •

It was quite therapeutic, submitting these diary entries. At the time, I thought that they would forever stand as a record for me to reflect on at some future date. Because, as we know, time can even dim the labour of childbirth.

The diary is a testament to the first year; not that the contact ceased to continue, but now the desperation has left me. The diary entries were followed up by a list of my recordings. I retrieved the disk with 'Chokas' on it and brought it into the lounge to document what was on it, followed up by laboriously going through my more recent recordings. It amounted to some forty-five recordings. This wasn't all of them, some still remaining on my 'phone downloaded quite badly. However, there were still some of the more extraordinary ones for him to listen to.

The remarkable thing about them is that most EVP consist of a very distorted, static, energetic sound with a few discernible words that the human ear is accustomed to picking up on. But 'Chokas', in particular, starts off with a sharp crack followed by a noiseless vacuum background and then the voice. I have requested that the recordings be somehow forensically fingerprinted for human voice patterns, because that voice alone evidenced for me the entire experience.

At the time of writing this book, the parapsychologist has commented that my experiences are "unusual", and he accepts that I have

encountered "something strange". This has left me somewhat perplexed as I had expected some more definite sort of result. The present
situation is not satisfactory because I have not moved on in any way,
nor has there been any conclusive answer. Maybe that is just the nature
of things.

But it did happen, it happened to me. I cannot change that and neither
can I alter how I feel about it. I invite others' opinions and investigations. [1]

---

[1] For those interested in pursuing their own study in this area, the most absorbing and
convincing research I have come across is that of Dr Rupert Sheldrake (author of The
Science Delusion). His work suggests that intelligent morphic fields are located in and
around the systems they organise, including human beings. It is difficult to summarise
the complexities of his work, most recently shedding light on telepathy and the nature
of the mind, but many feel that he may well ultimately be proven to have described the
most fundamental basis of life.

# 10
# The End of the Beginning

*'Every truth passes through three stages before it is recognised.*
*In the first place it is ridiculed. In the second it is opposed.*
*In the third it is regarded as self-evident.'*

—ARTHUR SCHOPENHAUER

This book could never have been published, had it not been for a series of synchronicities. It was through Clive's continuous encouragement and reminding me to log each and every event, communication or contact, as and when they occurred. The diary of communications grew alongside my confidence, constantly feeding my impoverished spirit. I was quite happy with this personal quest, neither distracted nor deterred by outside influences. I gloried in the new-found knowledge and learning, and the realisation that I could find nothing to contradict my conviction that contact could be and was made. Happy, that is, until 'Chokas' arrived.

Those who considered that I had deluded myself would be guilty of nothing more than not knowing me. They could be excused in light of the fact that they could not be as well-read. I myself have always enjoyed good argument and debate, when founded on someone else's exploration, insight and learning. At this juncture, it was fortunate that my counsellor's daughter had studied parapsychology. This indirectly facilitated my contact with the parapsychologist as I now required an educated overview of someone who had immersed themselves in questioning reality and related phenomena. My diary to date had formed the basis of quite a comprehensive journal, which I submitted to him. My discourses with him kept the topic extremely pertinent and alive, along with my ongoing communications with Andrew.

However, it was not until July 2012 that I came across a book writing competition, whilst on holiday. This was the only time I had perused the popular magazine shelves. I turned to Clive and informed him that I was going to write a book. With the assistance of my highlighted journal and diary entries, and indeed sound recordings, I hastily drafted a synopsis along with an opening chapter. The publisher acknowledged receipt of what was then my proposal. This prompted me to research the publisher, identifying him as a spiritual man, and I was further encouraged to make contact. I asked him simply who 'Chokas' was? Silly as this may appear on the surface, I had carried this enigmatic repartee for some time. The kindly comments and the few swift exchanges that followed convinced me to complete the project, resulting in this book, Tap Once for Yes, published by Local Legend.

Why me? And how did I do it? I don't believe for one moment that I am unique amongst mortals. People all around the world are experiencing the loss of a loved one. The relationships vary but I think that the contact is by and large determined by the depth of the bond. Maybe it is the pain, the trauma or the immediacy of the demise that provokes the intention and necessity to facilitate communication. I don't believe for one moment that you can just dial 'M' for Mother. If death is a natural process of nature and there is an affirmation of love prior to the separation, then perhaps there is less likelihood of contact. And, let us not forget, it is well documented that people experience the presence of their loved ones after death. It is normal to doctors that their patients relate these experiences; normal, but nevertheless not considered a reality, since anything unmeasured must be supernatural.

And yet the essence of the reality that science dictates is, in its extreme, as nonsensical in its argument as any paranormal activity. However, do not forget that paradigms shift. My own belief is that the intensity surrounding the detail of this story is testament both to

Andrew's desire and my own desperation to unite once more. The urgency with which Andrew had responded in our first communication was apparent, so definite and pronounced. So, ultimately, the bond you have and your openness are all that is required. Finally, you need not take my word for it; this contact is far more common than you the reader might realise, until you start to make your own enquiries. I for one would be very interested in your learning and feedback. And as Dave Allen, a very popular Irish comedian of a few years ago would say when closing his television shows, "May your god go with you."

Was I alarmed by my experience? Again I say, "I feel I know something, but I don't know what it is I know." But I have learned from my communication with Andrew that love is somehow the transcendent force behind the universal truth. You may consider that it is hatred that can indeed kill, maim and hurt. But the absence or withdrawal of love, that we see on a daily basis, can both destroy and disable with crucifying intensity.

Our loved ones continue to support us in a time and dimension not perceivable by us. I have further gleaned that this world merges with theirs, with subtlety. Their ability to communicate fluctuates in strength according to need. There are many questions that Andrew would not answer, and I have to question whether he is able to. Perhaps if we knew the answers, then some would be tempted to wander off this film set and go home to their loved ones.

I did ask Andrew from the beginning if he had met with Adam, his brother. At first, he was most insistent that he had only met my father, and then one day he communicated that he had met Adam and his dad's father.

Andrew has assured me numerous times that he is there if I need him. All through my darker moments, Andrew never failed to show support, his communications varying in strength between weaker and stronger responses, until Mothers' Day when he orchestrated a combination - the three very loud taps followed immediately by a tuneful drumming, ending with enormous effort "An... dr... eew"!

Quite often, and I suspect that it's when his energy permits it, or in the absence of our being able to have meaningful discourse other than through taps, Andrew now drums tunes, different ones. I feel that sometimes, when I try to draw him to answer the bigger questions, he responds simply by "Yes" (meaning, it is Andrew), followed by three taps to send his love.

There has been a glimpse of a divine essence that we can all access. The not knowing what it is, is down to the inadequacy of our language to express the nature of all that permeates our very existence. Spiritual and mystical interpretations differ wildly, and this I believe is largely down to subjective individuals striving to convey the unimaginable, limited as we are by our restricted senses. So for the genuinely gifted, and there are genuinely gifted people out there, and for enlightened individuals, the differing viewpoints and understanding can be forgiven. Not in the sense that they are not legitimate pictures or explanations of anomaly, but that their versions are inhibited by their own cultural archetypes, while still representing one integrated universal source.

For instance, can you have a thought without an image entering your mind, or vice versa? Are thoughts and images the same or are they different? Without language, could we still make sense of the world? Ancient languages were largely pictorial, based on images. For our ancestors, visual images were a language. A good example would be that a profoundly deaf person uses sign language, so for them words are a pale imitation of reality, whereas a pictorial language represents what actually is there in a much more accurate way.

When you look at a beautiful landscape, a complex fusion of images and thoughts assaults the senses, and any attempt to try and describe or quantify them does not do nature any justice. This I believe is the nature of spirit and spirit contact. The essence of this hidden invisible realm can leave its impression on our souls, leaving our waking selves with a deeply ingrained sense of knowing.

This brings me to what I feel I know and yet don't know! This feeling has haunted me from the outset, prompting my manic explorations and reading obsessions. It is a combination of all I have touched on and more. The truth and source is somewhere between the lines, and within all of us, a never-ending journey of fantastic proportions. I believe that time is a byproduct of this source being able to think about itself.

Andrew boarded a ship that day, one we shall all board. But I do know that when I arrive at the other end, Andrew will be there waiting, congratulating me on a journey well-travelled. And then perhaps we will wait a little while more to greet the next ship ....

• • •

The grief of losing someone can be the most chronic and disabling of pains, resulting in varying depths of depression affecting one's ability to function both physically and mentally, particularly when the loss is unexpected for whatever reason. The living emotional investment is terminated mid-flow. One's world view is changed within a beat of the heart. For the mother who has lost a child, at whatever age, the pain is raw, excruciating and unrelenting in the harrowing, ruthless void that is left.

Enough said. I cannot pretend to understand the many complexities and intricacies of someone else's grief process. It is certainly a bespoke, solo journey tailored and influenced only by the unfortunate individuals whose lives are impacted in the immediate now, or at some point in the future. The purpose of this book is not to prescribe alternatives or convince you of any revelation – the answers are intuitively yours. All I can do is share my own personal passage, and if by doing this it creates a catalyst for your own exploration, in your desire to seek solace, then my pen has been useful.

What is the nature of 'belief'?

I remember as a child of six, being on a swing in the garden and wondering why the adults were talking in hushed whispers. I had overheard that some relative had died, before being hastily ushered out into the garden to play. I remember feeling quite confused by this turn of events. My childish mind struggling to make sense of the obvious distress this had caused my parents as they busily catered to the small party of people that had congregated at the house.

My grandfather joined me to reassure himself that I was ok and I asked him to confirm my understanding of where we went when we died. I recall his careworn, sad face as he sat down beside me, explaining that everyone returned to 'God in Heaven' where everybody was happy and met with everyone they had ever loved. This satisfied me only a little, because even at that age I still could not understand why, if it was such a wonderful place, they were so unhappy? And if it was true, why were they so concerned that I might be knocked over by a car? The worst that could happen is that I could just play until they got here.

I was sent to Sunday School every week without fail, secure in the knowledge that if my parents knew the answer to life and death, then this sacred place confirmed it. However, there was something else about religion that perplexed my young mind. Hearing the sound of drums approaching accompanied by some brass instruments, I had excitedly run to secure a place on the pavement between the throngs of people that lined the road. My father had grabbed my small hand in his, firmly leading me away. This was Scotland, and the Orange Day parade was synonymous with religious division.

I was a Protestant and all my friends were, and that's why in my mind we had the best school and also the best of friends that could be had. Catholics were to be avoided if you came across them. I had been hit and smacked by a passing group of Catholics more than once. One particular child that hit me had a dimple in her chin, so from that moment on I thought that I and I alone knew that the secret to telling us apart was the differentiating dent in the chin, to be avoided.

I wondered why their God was different to ours. Was it because of their ignorance or did my parents maybe know more than theirs? I didn't really care, because that was their problem, but doubtless they would not share our Heaven. That was where all the good people went. I could not question this judgmental, all-knowing God.

I was nine years old when we moved to England. I found it disturbing to see a Catholic girl in my class and felt duty bound to ensure that everyone at least tried to know the difference. But the people in this country were not at all suspicious; they did not appear to have been taught as I had. Still, if my friends chose to consort with Catholics that was not my problem; but they could rest assured that they would not see them in Heaven.

Fortunately, I did eventually grow out of this philosophy and way of thinking. By the age of thirteen I became aware of a growing curiosity about religion. I attended a Young Christian movement. I was told by the elders of the movement that, when I was ready, I could ask God to come into my life and then – bang! I would be a real Christian. I knew the teaching and philosophy was integrally sound and good, and to be aspired to, but this only compounded my feelings of inadequacy. It left me frustrated that, unlike others around me, God did not appear to complete me – so there had to be something wrong with me. I was obviously not open enough to Him and my somewhat furtive child-like mind was not entirely attractive to Him. I tried so hard to be perfect, but could never achieve it.

I joined the British Army at the age of seventeen. The time inevitably came when I was posted to Northern Ireland. This country was a quagmire of irreconcilable differences between two opposing factions, the Protestants versus the Catholics. My memories of Scotland served to remind me of these ill-conceived conditioning ideas and responses indoctrinated into the malleable minds of children. I saw the damage inflicted, seeded and grown from the time they become aware of adult prejudices.

In Northern Ireland, duties were varied and some frequently routine. Some remain with me as all more profound memories do. I will outline one particular occasion (although there were many) which for me spotlighted the hypocrisy and futility of many exoteric (institutional) religious followers, which in some ways parallels present day conflicts.

It was Christmas when we arrived to carry out a house search in a salubrious area, at a beautiful house with expensive furnishings. The family, with two older teenagers, were obviously extremely angry at this eve of Christmas visit as we stood appraising the huge, ornately decorated tree. The abundant presents below it indicated that this was quite a wealthy household, promising an exciting day to come. I recall that in the corner, beneath a picture of the Sacred Heart, were ornate bottles of holy water and symbolic religious ornamentation. Nearby, thirty-two identical teddies, complete with seasonal ribbons, smilingly invited young hands to take them home; except that these teddies were to be packed with explosives… Merry Christmas.

Religions can destroy spirituality with their divide and rule mentality. Yet there is a widespread search for spirituality, a turning against materialism. Millions are on their own journey, quietly waking up to the real 'I', the awareness that has always been within.

I remember a Horizon TV programme about how much we actually miss in our day to day environment. The presenter was talking directly to the camera. Realising the nature of the programme, I concentrated on the scenery behind him. As he was speaking, a man dressed in a big fluffy bunny outfit passed from left to right, not once but several times. The object of this was to quantify the huge percentage of the viewing audience that had not indeed seen the bunny at all. Yet it could be seen by all those who were looking for it. A few other experiments along similar lines were also broadcast. Each and every time, both Clive and I always saw the anomalous addition. This was obviously a direct result of our not wanting to be distracted by what we would normally focus on. Therefore I would suggest that, if you are looking for the metaphoric fluffy bunny, you will see it.

Considering how much we don't know, it seems odd to me when the celebrated scientists of the moment, having a few pieces of the jigsaw, proceed to postulate quite assuredly about the remainder of its image. They don't seem to be thinking for one moment that, for example, the house surmised to be there could very well turn out to be a submarine or a monkey, or indeed both. There could be millions of possible outcomes. The point is, yes, one can describe the three pieces of the puzzle that one has, but finding, say, a wire does not automatically suggest it belongs to a television. Therefore, to my mind science doesn't seem to be any different to religion, both crediting their own particular God as the only source of possible truth, expressed within their own doctrines while ignoring the unknowable, the variable and the possible. Mainstream science suggests a form of atheism, which can be as damaging as any other radical stand that can be taken.

Being mainstream is rather like being an icon of the pop industry. It does not mean you are the best singer or the most talented, just that a lot of money is being made. Reality is obscured by mainstream media, made to resemble something more akin to children's entertainment and designed to distract and entertain the masses, but not to inform. Yet the masses are comprised of individuals who are striving to find more purpose to their lives, frustrated that what they are experiencing is still void of value. We are encouraged to buy into life, defining our happiness in terms of the next acquired possession - a life based on "I want this, how do I get it from you?" This only serves to make us temporarily 'not unhappy'.

I salute those who have gone out on a limb, at some cost perhaps to their careers, for what they believe true because, I think, that is certainly more likely to bring about a unification of science and religion.

My surmising is not entirely down to my focus on life after death study, which is obviously of real interest to me. But this has led me to other findings that are not mainstream, and that have the potential to revolutionise education and the analytical abilities of our forthcoming generations. It is this that captures my attention and rather excites me.

I have had some interesting conversations with people, obviously alluding to my experiences, who mention Derren Brown, the extraordinary mentalist and illusionist. I have watched his shows and am fascinated by how people can be fooled by his performances. I give him credit.

But people fail to recognise the biggest of illusions that they fall for. The entire world is governed and ruled by the huge mentalist efforts of presiding governments and policy makers. The world is as they portray it to us. The media, too, is controlled by a minority; this is not a conspiracy theory, it is fact. But this is territory that can upset the sensibilities of a large percentage of people, and with their assistance the illusion is kept intact and perpetuated.

I have pondered further that world leaders or leading politicians must have something of a sociopathic disposition, some more refined than others. If they didn't, they would not be able to sleep at night. Gone are the days when politics was pursued by the altruistic, now invariably replaced by power-hungry career politicians.

Scratch below the surface of any service or institution and you will usually find that it does not really work or run as it should, and it doesn't care as it should. But what our cultural leaders rely on and encourage is our unquestioning acceptance of the paradigms they have indoctrinated us into. They rely on our self-policing, on a consensus belief in reality serving only to bang our heads up a blind alley. It is our fear of the unknown that holds us back.

Why am I saying all this?

It is not just the rhetoric of a bereaved mother, but a direct result of over a year's undivided attention and focus on the fundamentals of existence. It is the realisation that what we thought we knew is primarily flawed. The real picture is hindered wherever there is evident self-interest. This takes the forms of individual academic egos, governmental interest, educational and societal control.

Love for one's offspring is the closest you get to forfeiting your own ego.

• • •

The question may arise in your mind that if I am so sure of my contact with Andrew, then could the recordings not be submitted for scientific analysis? I too was curious as to whether the parapsychologist could take the recordings apart acoustically. But it was suggested to me that, in the absence of video footage of the interactions, there was no way of determining absolutely the source of what I was hearing.

This did not sit satisfactorily with me. I couldn't grasp why. Surely an acoustic investigation (in terms of spectrum analysis) could bring about a conclusion? Eventually the day came when I had the opportunity to submit some sample files for preliminary investigation with an appropriate professional body.

Nervously, though confident, I awaited the feedback. I was told that in light of there being alleged paranormal communication, such investigation was incompatible with formal scientific methods. Put simply, the findings were inconclusive because there could be many and various scientific explanations of the phenomena. And any conclusions, apparently, could be inaccurate. Therefore, without a considerable amount of time and cost, "the investigation may be of little value ... "

I now consider this just an interruption of my own continuing investigations. However, all those professionals and educated or otherwise individuals, who have experienced paranormal phenomena of any sort, now have my sympathies. I take my hat off to those who remain unfaltering in their belief of personal experience, and to those of you who are reading this and who may one day experience the unexplained.

We are all of us imperfect observers in this world; we have such a limited range of perception. A good analogy would be that of doctors throughout the ages. There was a time when death was determined only by the absence of a beating heart, with no knowledge of the electrical activity of the brain. Therefore the doctor's determination could be wildly inaccurate. Delving into the fundamentals of our world requires the development of sophisticated instruments that can translate something beyond our normal capacity to understand into the right sort of impulses that can activate the sight, hearing and touch through which we interpret our world.

Even so, we have always to doubt the veracity of our technology, as it is still shaped by our intellectual imperfections and limitations, guided by theories that are not yet complete. Just because we fail to detect something is not evidence of its absence, rather that perhaps we do not have the right sort of instrumentation to translate it for our limited senses. Therefore the most important aspects of consciousness remain mysterious.

The mere fact that so many questions like this exist excites me greatly. Plato believed that "since the soul does not exist in time and space as the body does, it can access universal truths…"; and Descartes held that "the mind is distinct from matter, but can influence matter…", an interesting and inspiring concept in relation to quantum physics. The greatest strokes of genius in history have been inspired in the first instance by mind alone.

Where does religion fit in with this? I can no more answer that than any other question. But I do know that we have to treat it all with reverence. Because to do that is truly indicative of the awesome wonder in which we exist.

Kierkegaard said, "There are two ways to be fooled. One is to believe what isn't true, the other is to refuse to believe what is true."

Scepticism is a word that has been hijacked by fundamentalists. To be a sceptic used to imply an inquiring mind, an asking of questions. Today it would appear to be considered sceptical if one were to ridicule anything not compatible with one's belief system. Pyrrho, the original founder of Scepticism, intended it to be about open inquiry and suspension of judgment. A true sceptic seeks evidence, challenging both sides and including themselves and their own position in the equation.

So all I want to say to you is to remain powerful in your own convictions; it is too easy to be railroaded and almost mentally raped of any credibility. I know there are huge swathes of people out there who have confidentially related to me their own experiences of their departed, only to be thoroughly embarrassed when they have brought it to the attention of doctors, family and friends. Believe in yourself and your experience, bring it out of the proverbial closet and let's put it on the table. Give paranormal phenomena a chance and in doing so hopefully remove the supernatural element, allowing it to become acceptable in the mainstream.

• • •

This has been the most devastating year in my entire life and I continue to miss Andrew daily. Every day someone, somewhere, is experiencing the turmoil of bereavement, a life-changing moment for many. I hope my sharing of my journey and story can assist, inspire, support and soothe at what is a tumultuous time. I hope, for those of a more spiritual inclination, that it will reinforce their belief and understanding.

But above all, I hope this book will encourage and motivate the reader to undertake your own exploration, by investigating the less mainstream reading materials and thought-provoking ideas. It has never been my intention to convert or preach. But remember that the light burns at the edge of the shadows. Please undertake your own sceptical inquiry, in the truest sense of the word, by continuing to ask your own silly questions!